Call o
Twice Re

The Necessary and Unique Role for the African/Caribbean
in the Future of the Americas, Europe and Beyond

Amal Abdalhakim-Douglas

Black Stone Press & DMC Books

ISBN: 978-0-9535993-6-3 *(print edition)*

http://www.black-stone.net/books
http://www.amaldouglas.com

CONTENTS

	Page No.
Preface	5
The Twice Removed	13
An Interview With Ralston X (part 1) (A Nation Divided)	19
For the Coming Woman	31
An Interview With Ralston X (part 2) (Follow the Money)	45
The Role of the Market In Any Future African Economy	53
An Interview With Ralston X (part 3) (End of Apartheid)	71
Tassawuf - The Hidden Face of Africa	81
A New Islamic Money System for the 21st Century	101
NAGA Global Objectives	125
Pictures & Graphics	127
Selected Bibliography	128
More About the Author	130

Allah has blessed me with so many great teachers over the years, formal and informal, near and far. From my parents, siblings family and relatives, by both blood and marriage. My classmates & teachers, workmates, friends, *bredren* & *sistren* of years gone by. My Shaykh and my companions on the path. May **Allah** bless and be generous to every single one of you.

AUTHOR'S PREFACE

It's so very true that we cannot live or dwell in the past. Our time is now and our place is firstly, wherever we find ourselves, and secondly, wherever we might choose to locate ourselves if we are one of those lucky few able to make and act on that choice.

That said; It is often espoused (though of course never proven) that most people (both 80% & 90% are often quoted) die within 20 miles of where they were born. It is also commonly accepted that in normal circumstances people rarely move out of the economic or social class they were born into. It takes a rare individual with rare opportunities to break away from his or her **historical self**. In fact when Malcolm Gladwell in his book "Outliers", explains the real reasons for success behind so many names we may have heard about, it's not that they left their historical selves behind, but in fact it was their historical legacy that put them in a position to make use of what were relatively sparse opportunities.

World history is replete with lessons as will be our own family histories. Though in this work the focus is on the key lessons that are in some ways unique to, and that still impact on, those who can be included in the definition of the Twice Removed as described in the opening chapter.

This current work is a collection of articles all originally penned before the turn of the millennium. Some were published as stand alone articles and pamphlets, while some were contributions in other publications. Some of the predictions have proved true. Some proposed events took place while others morphed into something else. Some key players relocated, some fell away and some passed away. Therefore in some chapters it felt necessary to add an updating footnote that readers might find of interest or that would answer the most obvious questions that might arise.

In the context of this book our recent historical experiences have unfortunately more often than not included being at the sharp end. The sharp end of post-slavery colonialism, race politics and the later fight for independence. The sharp end of segregation and the civil rights movement. The sharp end of apartheid and the continuing exploitation of natural resources benefitting the former colonial masters and their inheritors.

The task before us is to firstly gain a true understanding of the historical context. Secondly we have to understand our own historical selves. Thirdly we have to understand our own individual and collective purpose, what we were created for. Only then can we make that necessary break from our historical selves and embrace the unique opportunities we have.

As ever many will enjoy reading **An Interview with Ralston X**. It's very easy to imagine sitting there and hearing it live on the radio for the very first time. However, here I need confess that Ralston X is in fact a fictional character and that the interview is a literary ploy. I say fictional but in truth the words are real, the sentiment even more so.

In many ways Ralston X represents a continuation of the path Malcolm X *might* have trodden, had he lived longer. The words are based on the words of so many real people who were around at that time and who I had the pleasure of meeting, interviewing and often working with at a later date. Almost everything else in the interview was also been said and done by real people I met and often knew well. The fact that it was originally written over 20 years ago is testament to its authenticity and the pedigree of those people and their understanding of how things would in fact evolve.

In reading **For the Coming Woman** you certainly should not read it as a criticism of the black woman. It's the opposite! It's a celebration and endorsement of those women who have understood, who have rolled up there sleeves and got on with it. The vocal feminist or self styled modern woman may "talk a good fight," but you really wouldn't want to have her in your corner. It's also a message to the emerging man. It's an indication to them of how to recognise and help develop a good woman and become the kind of man she needs and deserves.

In **Tassawuf - The Hidden Face of Islam in Africa** we draw heavily on the works of the great Shaykh Uthman dan Fodio of West Africa *as translated by (Hajja) Aisha Bewley.* Here the emphasis is on **Ihsan**, worshipping Allah as if you see him, taking on good qualities and moving away from bad qualities.

You have to know that you cannot build a society on the shariah. The shariah establishes legal limits but wherever the Deen of Islam was established and flourished the people lived by the sunna, that living example of that first dynamic community of Muslims in the illuminated city, Madina that included the Prophet Muhammad, peace & blessings be upon him, and their immediate followers. The practice was always to go above and beyond the requirements of the shariah in kindness, generosity, social welfare and civic responsibility. Shaykh Uthman reminds us how each of us can take this on in the modern age.

Although we quote heavily from Shaykh Uthman dan Fodio we have to remember that the beginning of the last century saw the continued weakening of the Sokoto Caliphate that he had established a century before that and which had dominated West Africa. Eventually its weakness would allow the region to fall to mainly British and French colonising armies.

Shaykh Abdalqadir as-Sufi reminds us in his **Letter to An African Muslim** the current state of affairs in that:

There is not one autonomous, self-governing state in Africa today. Where ownership and control lies we will examine later, Firstly we must look at the methodology that has been imposed on and is now functioning in the control of Africa by Alien forces.

Let us ask:

How is Africa controlled?
Why is Africa controlled?
What lies behind the control of Africa?

Only after we have examined the answers to those questions may we examine the road to freedom, and it is not Frantz Fanon's for he has been precisely one of the instruments of that ruthless control. Colonial methodology rests on five principles.

Shaykh Abdalqadir goes on to name the five principles as being:

1. The Partition Principle
2. The Linguistic Principle
3. The Democracy Principle
4. The Minority Principle
5. The National Myth Principle

It is beyond the scope of the present work to examine these principles in detail but the destabilising effect of each of them is mentioned repeatedly throughout.

We finish by positing **A New Islamic Money System for the 21st Century** you'll come to realise that we could just as easily have called it an *African, Caribbean, Debt Free* or *Non-Usurious* money system. Everything that we mention concerning banks and the necessity for using gold and silver has now become common knowledge and accepted logic. We have to begin to assess every situation, every war, every *coup d'état* by following the money. Who is making money from this turmoil, this war, this instability?

However, many still miss the point. Some still talk of **reparation** as something that will right past wrongs and redress imbalances, but reparation is what the losers pay the victors. If you use the victors paper money, have arrangements in place where they continue to reap the benefits of your natural resources to the detriment of the local populace and willingly or otherwise, adopt their corrupted styles of governance and administration, then reparation is not on the cards. In any case the likelihood is that it would not make an iota of difference. What you need to do in these circumstances is get your own house in order at both a local and national level. At the heart of this will be a tangible **currency**, fair commercial **contracts** and an infrastructure that facilitates access to **markets** at home and abroad for everyone with a desire to trade, whether on a small or larger scale. *A New Islamic Money System* goes some way to explaining how to go about doing this wherever we are.

The Jamaican poet Vera Bell captures some of the sentiment we are trying to illicit in her classic 1948 poem:

Ancestor on the auction block
Across the years your eyes seek mine
Compelling me to look.
I see your shackled feet
Your primitive black face
I see your humiliation
And turn away
Ashamed
Across the years your eyes seek mine
Compelling me to look
Is this mean creature that I see
Myself?
Ashamed to look

Because of myself ashamed
Shackled by my own ignorance
I stand
A slave
Humiliated
I cry to the eternal abyss
For understanding.

Ancestor on the auction block
Across the years your eyes meet mine
Electric
I am transformed
My freedom is within myself.
I look you in the eyes and see
The spirit of God eternal
Of this only need I be ashamed
Of blindness to the God within me
The same God who dwelt within you
The same eternal God
Who shall dwell
In generations yet unborn.

Ancestor on the auction block
Across the years
I look
I see your sweating, toiling, suffering
Within your loins I see the seed
Of multitudes
From your labour
Grow roads, aqueducts, cultivation
A new country is born
Yours was the task to clear the ground
Mine be the task to build.

The Twice Removed

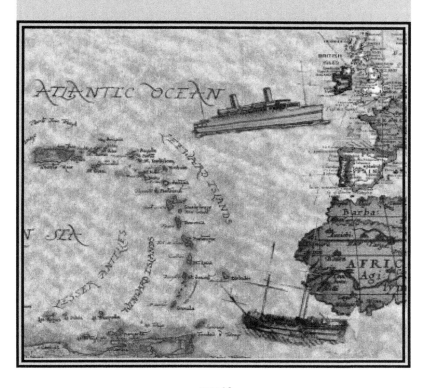

That "second removal," that mass migration from the Caribbean colonies of young men and women coming to help the 'motherland', to make their way in life and even to make their fortune. Coming to be labourers, craftsmen. nurses, cooks and cleaners. Others came as administrators, entertainers and entrepreneurs. They came as British citizens with British passports from countries that were still part of the British empire. *(In America there would be a corresponding movement from South to North)*

You can't reverse mass migration, not even through draconian laws and the evils of mass deportation or genocide. You can dilute, you can discriminate, you can even manipulate public opinion to turn against and become hostile to the later arrivals but you can't reverse it.

However, let me pause lest making the classic mistake of forgetting that this migration that gained so much momentum in the post World War II late 1940's through to the 1960's was really just part two of that "second removal." Part one begins in earnest with World War I, that unnecessary slaughter of so many young men in particular.

Many of these personnel came from the Caribbean (and other parts of the British empire). A great number would settle in Britain both while serving and as ex-servicemen. Perhaps the best I can do here is refer readers to take a look at Stephen Bourne's well researched work: **Black Poppies - Britain's Black Community and the Great War.**

In 1914 Britain was home to at least 10,000 black Britons, many of African and West Indian heritage. Most of them were loyal to the 'mother country' when the First World War broke out. Despite being discouraged from serving in the British Army, men managed to join all branches of the forces, while black communities contributed to the war effort on the home front.

By 1918 it is estimated that Britain's black population had trebled to 30,000, as many black servicemen who had fought for Britain decided to make it their home. It was far from a happy ending, however, as they and their families often came under attack from white ex-servicemen and civilians increasingly resentful of their presence. With first-hand accounts and original photographs, Black Poppies is the essential guide to the military and civilian wartime experiences of black men and women, from the trenches to the music halls.

Of course there has been a documented black presence in Britain for many hundreds of years but again, that is a different matter.

In terms of the "first removal" we are referring to that forced migration out of the continent of Africa and into the Americas, the Atlantic Slave Trade. On this subject also a lot has been said and there are of course differing views on the extent or nature of African involvement at both its beginning and end. Again, there is no reversal, no going back. For many left on the continent they would also face their own removals of a different kind. From traditional and ancestral lands, from ways of worshipping their Creator, from ways of working earning a livelihood and from traditional forms of governance. In many situations these removals would have been no less traumatic.

Through this legacy there are so many of us black people with African blood running through our veins yet now mixed with Indian, Native American/Amerindian, Chinese, European and Arab blood. Yet despite the passage of time and so much mixing the words sung by Peter Tosh still ring true:

"No matter where you come from, so long as you're a black man, you're an African...."

For many of us that recognition of our heritage meant we wanted the best for "our people." We wanted to be both the true companions to, and inheritors from, Walter Rodney, Marcus Garvey, Malcolm X, George Padmore, Edward Blyden, Kwame Toure et al. Therefore it had to take us beyond immature notions of the white man being the devil, beyond the rhetoric of everything African is good, beyond the paradigms of democracy *vs* dictatorship or capitalism *vs* socialism. If it was correct and good it had to pass the test of being good and correct for everyone who embraced it, and even those that didn't.

Just becoming Muslim itself was still not enough. It meant gaining a true understanding of the society and times we live in and how it should function socially, economically and politically. It meant being brave enough to go back to the roots of Islam, rejecting the later distortions of *wahabism* on one extreme, the *shia* on another, and a hypocritical *ultra-modernists* movement on yet another. It meant going into, and if necessary, through Pan-Africanism, taking on anything that was good and true while rejecting what was merely an emotional distraction.

It often meant uprooting our families and moving to places where we could begin to put what we had learned into action, even if only at a seemingly micro level. It meant taking charge of our own affairs as best we could.

If our story is still being written then what follows constitute the opening chapters. Your challenge is to write an appropriate ending.

An Interview with Ralston X
(part 1)

Gus Westcott's interview with Ralston X

PART 1

The following is the full transcript of an interview by WCLX's Gus Westcott with Ralston X otherwise known as Uthman Malik Abdal Hakim. The interview was the first public speech given by Ralston X since 1981 and took place at the studios of WCLX and was broadcast live on December 3 1993. Despite numerous requests WCLX have refused to release audio or written copies of this interview contrary to their normal practice. This transcript was made from a listeners personal copy.

Gus Westcott: My guest today is the renowned Pan Africanist and Muslim activist Ralston X otherwise known as Uthman Malik Abdal Hakim, formerly a member of the Nation of Islam under the honorable Elijah Muhammad and also founding member of the Organisation of Afro American Unity or OAAU along with the more popularly known Malcolm X. Firstly Brother Ralston let me welcome you to the studios of WCLX FM and say how honoured I am to have you on the Show.

Ralston X: Thank you, I'm honoured to be here.

Gus: I'd like to first set the scene a little bit for some of our younger listeners. You were actually born in Brooklyn New York but your parents were from the Caribbean Islands.

X: Well my father was from Tobago and my mother from Guyana:

Gus: OK. You actually spent several years at school in Guyana before returning to the United States. You became a member of the Nation of Islam in 1963 under the Honourable Elijah Muhammad and subsequently split from the Nation along with Malcolm X.

X: Actually some time before Malcolm X along with many others.

Gus: Yes precisely. Then you helped form Muslim Mosque Incorporated and also the Organisation of Afro American Unity or OAAU. Since then the public details of your life have been very sketchy and you seem to have purposely shunned any publicity. What I would like to do is talk about your time in the Nation of Islam and your relationship with the Honorable Elijah Muhammad, with Malcolm X and with the present leader Minister Louis Farrakhan.

X: I think it is more important to talk about the present and the steps we need to take to turn our own situation around. Books have been written and films have been made around the life of Malcolm X and Elijah Muhammad and claims and counter claims have been thrown around since even before 1965, so people have had plenty of time and plenty of information from which to form opinions. I am not here to challenge anyone's opinions on Malcolm X or the Nation of Islam.

Gus: Does this mean you do not see eye to eye with Minister Farrakhan?

X: It means I have not, set eyes, on Mr. Farrakhan for nearly twenty years, and am therefore not in a position to comment on his, or the Nation of Islam's current activities.

Gus: Then does this mean you no longer have friends who are currently involved with the Nation of Islam?

X: No. It means that over the years people change and there outlook changes. It means that as our thinking matures so does our outlook on life and we begin to see deeper and deeper below the surface and we begin to see what the real issues are. Therefore ones conversations mature and there is little room for chit chat on the day to day runnings of the Nation of Islam or any other such group. They are a well known group with a large following and excellent recruitment techniques, and in fact I would urge any of your interested listeners to find where they meet and go and hear what they have to say. I think that they will find their meetings are never dull and even sometimes informative, but I think we should move on to more important matters.

Gus: I think you've made your position quite clear and thank you for that. Let me then ask you. Is there anything you can add or clarify concerning the death of Malcolm X, that is not already common knowledge?

X: Again let me say there is a wealth of available information for those truly interested, so any clarity must be about the time since Malcolm X, myself and others formed Muslim Mosque Incorporated and later the Organisation of Afro American Unity.

Gus: So this is the point when it was no longer seen as a religious struggle but a civil struggle?

X: What people have to realise is that we were Muslims and we were convinced Islam held all the answers for us, but we also realised that there were some very important principles we had to work with all the time. **One**, We had not been taught the true Islam of the Prophet Muhammad, peace and blessings be upon him. **And two**, That in our situation we were not in a position to or did we want to, impose any kind of religious or moral code on anyone. Also after much study we realised that a serious and unbiased look at Africa, especially West Africa held the key to a lot of what we needed to know. Therefore as a result of this we began to thoroughly research African History.

Gus: and what were your main discoveries?

X: Islam

Gus: Can you be more specific?

X: Well it's a fact that West African history over the last one thousand years is for the main part a history of the spread of Islam in Africa. No one can deny this so those who are serious will have to address this point at some stage. It doesn't mean people must become Muslims. It means people must understand how and why it spread, how and why it declined and what it produced, and what it did or didn't do for the people.

Gus: Is this then the reason why Malcolm X visited Africa and the Arab states?

X: All these things would have been a major influence

Gus: Did you visit any of these places yourself?

X: Not at that time, but since then I have spent a lot of time traveling between different communities in different countries, but as far as Malcolm X is concerned I believe that what motivated him was simply his persistence in pursuing the truth and acting according to it.

Gus: Would you say that this is the greatest lesson we could learn from him.

X: What I believe are the most important things that anyone who wishes to emulate Malcolm X need to take on are one, his integrity. In that I mean the fact that he would move from one position to that of a better one once he discovered that there was something higher and better to aspire to and so he died striving towards the best goal he thought man could aspire to. One thing I heard Malcolm say on many occasions was that adults could learn a great lesson from children which was not to be afraid of failure but to always get up and try again. That's why I'm sure if he had lived longer it wouldn't have taken him long to reach the position we have reached today in terms of analysis of our time and the way to deal with it. But I think that he was a man of tremendous character and he always strived to perfect his character and that is the lesson we should all begin to take on today.

Gus: Did he have a special method of this trying to perfect his character?

X: There are many aspects to good character which include loyalty, integrity, honesty, good timekeeping, finishing what you start, sticking to your word, generosity and other things that one can imagine. At the time Malcolm X was killed we had just come to realise that all these qualities we desired had been manifested in the Prophet Muhammad, peace and blessings be upon him. So that is where we had begun to take our example from and many people realised this.

Gus: Continuing on the topic of travel. On your own travels you must have met many interesting people and learned much that you would like to see implemented here in America?

X: Yes I have met some tremendous and interesting people from all walks of life.

Gus: I'm going to ask you about some of those people but first are there any people that you dislike meeting?

X: Politically you know I can't answer that.

Gus: Alright no specifics just the kind of questions they ask?

X: There are a set of people who call themselves a mixture of socialists, revolutionaries and Pan Africanists. Now there is nothing necessarily wrong with these titles or indeed people who follow these philosophies, but there are a section of them who think that they are, what they actually are not.

Gus: You mean the people themselves are not what they think themselves to be?

X: Yes

Gus: In what sense?

X: There are some of them who have a whole bag of rhetoric about Africa and don't have a clue about how the majority of Africans actually live. Then they take some of Africa's finest sons and totally distort what these people were about. So in effect what they propagate is actually not only totally alien to traditional African culture but would actually destroy Africa.

Gus: Are you making reference to anyone in particular?

X: You mean in terms of who's lives they distort?

Gus: Yes, but also what they propagate.

X: The most obvious and common examples are Marcus Garvey, Kwame Nkrumah and Malcolm X.

Gus: What would you say is the actual nature of this distortion of the lives or philosophies of these people?

X: I'll give you an example. I met a man in London England some years ago by the name of Bashir Kwanzaa who used to be the Foreign Minister, or what we would call Foreign Secretary, in the government of Kwame Nkrumah. What struck me was that I had recently attended a so called black Nationalist stroke socialist conference in which they had been claiming to be following a path of *Toureism\Nkrumahism* based on the philosophies of Sekou Toure and Kwame Nkrumah. At the time these people were totally dismissive of any role Islam had to play in Africa.

However when I met this man Bashir Kwanzaa who is a

Muslim he told me that he had not always been a Muslim, in fact he had been a Roman Catholic. Naturally I asked what had been the main cause behind him taking this step to the truth and he told me that one day Kwame Nkrumah asked him to go and study Islam. Naturally he was surprised and asked, why him, considering he was a catholic? He told me that Nkrumah replied "because Islam is the future of Africa. Islam is the future of Africa" I recall this story not to tell people to become Muslims, but to make the point that If you respect anyone that much then don't just take one isolated sentence out of a whole life and try to make a whole philosophy around it, but try to find out what they were aiming for, what they knew and sometimes more importantly what they didn't know.

Gus: You mean try and find out what the complete strategy would have been had they got that far.

X: Yes it's almost like your teacher going through a twenty chapter book but they died after only reaching chapter twelve. So what these people would do is stick at chapter twelve and never go any further, but what we have to do is take up the book with our fellow students, follow any notes your teacher left and go as far as you can until you can find a new teacher.

Gus: That's absolutely fascinating and I know that when I myself began to seriously study the life of Marcus Garvey I noted some very interesting Islamic connections also. Now obviously you would not be recommending anybody to join the type of group or people you so vividly described but are there any interesting groups around at the moment you could tell us about or that you would urge people to join?

X: I really would not like to encourage people to join specific groups unless they find that they and the people in that group actually share specific goals or ambitions. I would prefer like minded people to come together and learn from the best of those other groups.

Gus: What about your own movement, are there specific things you would like to pass on from your own experiences?

X: Well amongst the groups I'm closely affiliated with there is lot which we could put into practice here, especially and most importantly the appointment of Amirs from amongst ourselves.

Gus: Could you explain what an Amir is?

X: To put it very simply, an Amir is someone empowered by a group of people to be their leader and then the people who empower him also give him their loyalty, trust and obedience. So it's about people choosing someone they know to be the one who leads, not like what happens today when a fraction of the population vote for someone they have never met or even set eyes on to be there so called political representative.

Gus: So you are saying that this is a traditional form of Islamic Governance?

X: I am saying more than that, I'm saying that this is a traditional form of African governance which was the pattern wherever there were successful communities, and this is one of the things we discovered by taking an honest and unbiased look at traditional forms of African leadership.

Gus: If this is true which I don't doubt, then can you explain why Muslim countries such as Saudi Arabia and Pakistan, and African countries such as Zimbabwe or even Nigeria do not conform to this view?

X: I don't claim to be an expert on international affairs but it is clear that Pakistan has simply followed the pattern of its former colonial master England or Britain which is completely alien to Islam and even to the East Asian people and the results are obvious, and the same can be said of Zimbabwe. In fact in the Gulf war the Pakistani government sided with the American forces but the Pakistan soldiers sided with the people of Iraq. This is clearly a government that does not represent the people, much like we have in America today. As for Saudi Arabia this just exposes the hypocrisy of countries like this one and their crusade for democracy. It's obvious that because of the oil wealth in Saudi Arabia and the fact that the regime there is totally subservient to the wishes of the West that no one really gives a damn if there is democracy or not.

Gus: Nigeria?

X: What I've just said probably all relates to Nigeria in some way but really we need a whole program to discuss Nigeria. You see Nigeria is effectively at least two distinct and very different countries, the North and the South, but effectively what has been done is that all the real Amirs have been wiped out and replaced with people who are no more than puppets who parade themselves on public holidays. If one really would like to understand this further I suggest reading a book called Letter to An African Muslim by Shaykh Abdalqadir al Murabit it explains this scenario clearly.

Gus: We will come to books later, but are you saying that the current Muslim leaders have betrayed their people? In fact, lets take a break and come back with that question.

For the Coming Woman

For the Coming Woman

The totality of this message can only be recognised by those women who know they are women, and who know that the roles of the man and the woman are sometimes different. This is for the woman who knows it is incumbent on her to learn, to seek knowledge, to act according to that knowledge, and to also transmit that knowledge. This is for the woman who knows what a great responsibility we have towards our children so that their lives do not become meaningless and wasted. If you are not this woman then it is unlikely you will even finish reading the next paragraph.

Before we proceed let us throw out a word that always provokes either an inward or outward response from the modern black woman. Your reaction will most likely be based on media hype, fear, or just plain, but understandable ignorance. The word is Islam. Now if you are looking for this to be a defense of polygamy you will be disappointed because that is not the issue. In fact it is not even interesting. Anyone interested in that can go and tour the length and breadth of Africa and see it in action, or stay here and see the opposite in action, but what we want to discuss here are practical things that you can grasp on to and that make a difference. So let us now proceed.

We begin by acknowledging that our Creator is one and that at the end of this life each of us, individually, will answer to this Creator. If the black woman accepts this and remembers she will die, then and only then is she a conscious black woman. This conscious black woman is already head and shoulders above any woman who denies this reality, this truth. That woman is not conscious, she is asleep and her heart is dead. She is not interesting, she is a burden. She likes to talk and get involved in meaningless debates that never result in meaningful action. She is wasting her time we will not let her waste ours.

Now the conscious black woman needs to become the wise black woman. For her this is easy. She uses her intellect and her spirituality, that inward connection to her Creator. In every situation she applies what she knows, makes the best decision she can, and then acts accordingly. More important however, is the fact that she learns from the decisions and the actions she takes. We will call this conscious and wise woman, the Coming Woman.

The coming woman will not dwell on the legacy of the Atlantic slave trade, she already knows the position the black woman finds herself in all over the planet. She will also already know of the wonderful quality of life some of those before us enjoyed when they lived as the Creator has prescribed. She will no doubt inwardly yearn to recreate a situation of such nobility for herself and her children. However, she is also interested in understanding how it is we have fallen victims to a new slavery arising out of a combination of jewish commercial techniques and christian defenselessness, apathy and collusion.

What we must do now is begin to analyse the society we live in and what it has to offer the coming woman. This process begins with the realisation that slavery has not finished, it never did finish, only the form has changed. If you depend on a salary to pay your mortgage, your rent, buy food or whatever else salaries are used for, you are a slave, a slave to your salary and the system that provides it, a wage slave. You have to toe the line. You are caught up in this endless cycle of nine to five, four weeks holiday, seeking promotion, hating the boss and maybe striving for a pension, while your own children are being cared for by some other wage slave. Are you beginning to see the similarity to life on the plantation? Maybe you sign on the dole (welfare), or if not you, the father or fathers of your children. This is even worse but it's all part of the same thing. The system that pays you needs to keep you in check.

We work harder and harder and yet still our money buys less and less. Africa and the Caribbean, full of natural resources, yet our people have less money than even we in Europe and America have. Someone somewhere, is manipulating the supply, value and destination of the money we use. It is all a result of monopolistic, corrupt and unfair commercial practices along with the unlimited creation of what is in reality false money, which is sanctioned by the State and exploited by the banks and other financial parasites that produce nothing. This is called usury and it is the root cause of incurable inflation, unemployment and endemic poverty across the globe. It is no wonder we make no progress economically. The State and the banks decide what our money can buy. If we make enough noise we will get another black woman MP or senator, and a few more prominent black faces who have no power to change anything. In other words the barking dogs get thrown a few more scraps from the table but will never be invited to eat at the table. The black man is beginning to wake up to the recognition of this slavish sickness, rejecting the scraps and seeking the real food, but unfortunately some women still accept what their men reject.

Look within our own homes look at all the problems we have there, all the arguments we have there, and what is at the centre of it; guilt and resentment. A woman is not supposed to live a life of domestic and emotional frustration, money problems, antidepressants, dead end love affairs, counseling, more babies and more guilt. A man who is willing and able to work and strive for his community is not supposed to be living a life of economic and political impotency, ending up in compulsive womanising, gambling, wife beating, crime or some useless job. The point we are driving at is that everything we have mentioned so far is all part of the same sickness of our time, and before we accept the remedy we have to admit we are sick. We are not deviating from the topic, but we cannot do anything positive while we are ignorant of the society we live in. We are going to set out below the practical steps we need to take, but we have to make sure that we really understand this question of the State and its far reaching effect right into our homes and upon our families.

We have to understand that there has been a complete

turn around in the running of the household, the home. Whenever a society flourished the woman had her own agenda and she ran it from the home. It was always a hive of activity and production, a place where things happened. If you think we mean a programme of cooking and cleaning you have missed the point. You are confusing it with what you see around you today. What we are talking about is the woman's space, to do what she needs to do, how she wants to do it. If she wants to run a business she runs it from there, the home is not the place for men, the men have their own programme and their own arena. The new woman needs to reclaim her space. She needs to tell her man; "Let me run things here, you go and find the men who are doing what needs to be done. I will be with the women, we have things that have to be done." Then we will begin to have real men and real women.

Today the home is an isolated box, a centre of consumption. Everything gets thrown into it and nothing comes out. We spend on the mortgage, food, electricity, gas, telephone and a host of electronic 'necessities' (television, stereo etc). Then when we are at home our time is consumed in the shallow escapism of watching the television, listening to dance music, playing video games and the like. There is now nothing attractive about the home, no inspiration or true culture can be drawn from it. We cannot even teach our children table manners because we prefer to sit in front of the TV with a polystyrene container from the local takeaway, yet we ourselves know better because many of our own parents embodied it. So we must keep in our minds the importance of the household and what happens there.

We must begin to take it upon ourselves to transform the home and our view of it, in order to accommodate the needs of this independent, and new woman.

Let us end on the current system of education, or you may already call it *miseducation*, that's a good start, but only a start. You will by now have realised that the current education system is only fit for producing wage slaves and robotic consumers. What we also have to realise is that sending our children to a top private school is not the answer, it just means that they will be higher up on the wage slave ladder, but nonetheless still slaves. They used to be called overseers. This does not mean we must not study mathematics, science, languages etc. It means we must think carefully, very carefully, about how and where we educate our children because we know that an oppressor or slave master will not show you the road to freedom. He will hide it from you and deceive you. Therefore we must ourselves firstly learn the science of living, embody it for our own protection, and then our children will learn from our own way of life. The woman is the child's first teacher because she is a woman of action, and children learn from actions, they learn by example.

Conclusion

Our belief is that every man and woman should, to the best of their ability, be pursuing the establishment of justice as it has just been defined. We believe that the first step for anyone must be recognition of the Creator and His prophets. This has to be a recognition that the

Creator, ALLAH, has power over everything and in comparison we have no real power. Therefore if we surrender to this reality we can then, and only then begin to achieve success.

The next step is to find a set of like minded and positive people to form the basis of community with clear leadership, a community made up of men, women and children who now begin to administer their own affairs in accordance to the way prescribed by the Creator which is known as the Shari'ah (the road). This means we do not need MPs to represent us we have our own from amongst ourselves.

If we get this far it means we will be in a position to see the real cause of all the social problems we are faced with today, usury. You the coming woman, will have to find out the real meaning of this word because it is deep, and it is evil, and we are all entangled in it, but it goes beyond the banks and interest and is either directly or indirectly responsible for every evil thing that we have mentioned so far. To explain it you must know that the sacred house in Mecca is the direction Muslims face when they pray. You must know that the Messenger of Allah (peace be upon him) says usury is not only seventy times more evil than a man committing incest with his own mother, but seventy times more evil than committing incest with his own mother in the said Sacred house. So if you understand what has been said so far you must now find the people who know, and learn from them the true meaning of this word usury.

If you are still with us we say Alhamdullilah (all praise

is due to ALLAH). You have something, you are healthy. Insha Allah (by the will of ALLAH) you will grasp onto what we have to say and things will become clear to you, and continue to become clear.

Justice, Social Justice. This is the issue, the establishing of just societies where people are free. The only restriction: do not exceed the boundaries set by ALLAH. Everything else is permissible. Wherever justice was in place, our communities always flourished. No argument. This was always the Islamic society. This issue is not new, every prophet from Adam through to Abraham, Moses, Jesus and Muhammad (peace and blessings be upon them all) came to establish justice and create just societies. It's about implementing what is fair and just, and none knows more about this than the Creator, It's about putting the right people in the right places and therefore choosing the best amongst us to lead us. Anything else is injustice.

It sounds like a heavy task but it's not, you just take one step at a time and the rest will follow, but you have to remember whenever anything positive happened amongst our people anywhere, it began with a small community, a firm belief, a clear vision and positive action.

What you have to do is find the people who are acting in accordance with what you have just learnt. They will be a community with a clear leader; there will be men, women and children; they will have a clear grasp of current issues and not be fooled by what is on the TV or in the newspapers; the women will see each other regularly and support each other; but of significant importance will be that the men stand out. Their time will be spent involving themselves in trading and in serious and positive action. They will have little time for frivolous pursuits. You will also notice that they keep talking about land, the need for land, the need for markets and the need for people to trade using real wealth and real money as opposed to bits of paper or plastic.

So we have come to the end, but for you it should be a beginning. You know the situation, you recognise the sickness, you recognise the cure and you know how to recognise the people. Now all you have to do is find them, join them and go forward together with them, Insha Allah.

Appendix: Looking Back - *from the not too distant future*

It may seem hard to believe now but in the late 20th / early 21st century women were often required to work side by side and competing with men in the workplace. It was a strange time when the anti-family, feminist movement, was fully entrenched and homosexuality and lesbianism although obviously not the norm were rampant and being foisted upon the masses as something normal. Many women chose to dress as slave women dress today, openly exposing much of their body. Indeed those women who tried to dress modestly as free women do today were often ridiculed in order that they didn't become role models. It was a very unhappy time for western women. Polygamy was outlawed so many women were forced to suffer the indignity of being mistresses with no legal protection. Fornication and adultery were not even considered as crimes or punishable in any way.

To earn a living many women would turn to what were seen as mild forms of prostitution such as sport, modeling, singing or acting. In these professions the women were often required to dress in the equivalent of knickers and a bra and do things like running, jumping, dancing, singing or in some cases even simulating sexual acts in front of a large television or live audience that included men, women and more often than not, children. The more lewd the act or the acting role, the greater the acclaim. Although considered "well paid" these women led largely unhappy lives and were exploited ruthlessly. Drug and alcohol addiction, eating disorders, and mental problems were commonplace amongst them. Women working in offices often admitted to "sleeping' their way to the top in order to get promotion but didn't consider this prostitution.

It was a time when young women were opting to climb mountains, cycle around continents and sail single handedly around the world but didn't know how to make up their beds in the morning or the first principles of running a household or worse still, the rudiments of personal hygiene, much less how to be a teacher to her children and a wife to her husband.

These were strange and confusing times for women.

In America the black man in particular, but real men in general, continued to be an endangered species with close to two million of them in jail and single mother parents were being portrayed as the norm.

The myth of democracy had been shattered by the election of a president by fraudulent means, corruption and the strategic denial of the right to vote for many of its citizens. Added to that, Americans had been forced to support wars against unheard of peoples they knew nothing about in order to protect the once mighty duo of the bankers and the US Dollar. Of course with hindsight we wonder how people could have been silly enough to have accepted printed bits of paper and computer digits as money, but these were strange times, people believed what they were programmed to believe, particularly in the West. To question anything was to be branded insane or even a terrorist of some sort. Terrorism was a re-invention of the time that kept the public in fear and legitimised wholesale murder and pillage on a huge international (not excluding the domestic) scale by the ruling elite, using other people's children to do the dirty work.

At that time western Europe was no better. Without a huge influx of immigrants countries like Britain and Germany could not survive, but in a culture of two-facedness, hypocrisy and double standards the local population were fed enough newspaper and television headlines to let them believe these newcomers would take their jobs, their houses, their money and their hospital and university places. It was a sad and corrupt time when only the lowest of the low became politicians.

The church was long since dead and had become a laughing stock with openly homosexual priests and regular reports of child molestation making the news. To not approve of sodomy or to pretend that a jew a Muslim, a Chinese an Arab, Buddhist, Black, White, Sodomite, man or woman were not the same and all equal, even though this defied the natural laws of logic was to be accused of racism, bigotry, homophobia, islamophobia, anti-semitism or worst of all 'intolerance.'

Tolerance was the new religion. You could be anything so long as you tolerated every corruption and most of all you had to tolerate every evil of the, then dominant, usurious financial system. A system that was itself complete insanity coupled with greed, and was behind almost every act of genocide, war, terrorist action and financial sanction that led millions to die from starvation, wars and diseases around the world.

Thank God that amongst all of that there were a group of people calling to the truth, calling us to redefine our family structures, to abandon the usurious financial system, to start using gold and silver as currency, to choose our own leaders from amongst ourselves, to take charge of our own and our children's education and most of all to completely surrender our will and worship Allah.

The rest, as they say, is history.

La hawla wa la Quwatta Ilah billah

An Interview with Ralston X

(part 2)

PART TWO

Gus: You were talking before the break about Muslims previously being betrayed by their leaders, but what about the current state of affairs.? There are lots of Muslim countries around the world.

X: What I am clearly saying is that there has been a global betrayal which has the majority of the world's population enslaved to a system based on pure myth and that at this time I know of no country which is exempt from this masonic control system.

Gus: What exactly is this myth.

X: Well part of the myth is that bits of paper called banknotes are actually real money.

Gus: So it sounds like you are an advocate of going back to the gold standard and linking the value of the dollar to gold.

X: It goes much further than that. We have to begin to reject the whole banking system and begin to trade using currencies with real value such as gold and silver, for while we chase bits of paper the bankers and their allies are grabbing the gold and the land and everything else of real value.

Gus: It's coming across as though you are totally at odds with the state of society and the democratic system of electing leaders and would like to replace it with something more community based. Am I right?

X: What I would say is to look at South Africa. We are

reportedly four months from an historic election yet still everyone knows the ANC is going to win and Nelson Mandela will be president. Now you may think the reason we know this is because the ANC and Nelson Mandela are so popular. The truth is there are many other groups with arguably much more credibility than the ANC but those who control the media have not chosen them to be the new overseers they've chosen Mr. Mandela and all the Jews and Indians that make up the ANC. Now if you look closely enough you'll find people like McMillan Book publishers have already signed major contracts with the ANC in advance of any election, and the more you look the more corruption you will see. The truth is that the South African banks have run out of people to enslave in the debt trap of mortgages and loans and it's time to pick the ripe fruit of over thirty million black people just there for the taking.

Gus: You certainly have a clear and even unique critique of the current world political and economic situation. Is this now a common understanding among Muslims or are you still very much a minority voice even amongst the Muslims?

X: I think that most people whether Muslim or not know that there is something fundamentally wrong with the way we have been forced to live today, and there are many individuals and groups who voice concern over these matters. In particular I can think of those affiliated to the League of the Black Stone movement both here in America and also in Africa, Europe and the Caribbean, and there is also the European based Murabitun movement amongst others. Both these groups have written much material on the myth of the world banking system and the control the international financiers have over all of our lives.

Gus: Unfortunately time won't permit us to delve into these matters sufficiently but I do know that this is a very important and interesting topic.

X: On the contrary, as you said these are important matters and I think that your listeners deserve at least that much respect to once in a while here a discussion on topics that are real and have such a total and devastating effect on all our lives.

Gus: OK what I propose is that we come back to what I agree are very important matters in the last half of the show. However you did mention books and normally on this show I like my guests to recommend three books to our listeners, and I'm sure you can come up with an interesting selection.

X: Sounds like pressure from the producer?

Gus: Lets just say it's getting hot but we will continue on this theme. I'm sure you'll be the first to agree that we could spend a whole programme on these matters but maybe the books you suggest may actually cover these very matters.

X: I'll go with that but I'll have to think a little about the books, but first one has to remember that books contain information and not knowledge. Knowledge only comes through action, by doing something, but on saying that I would definitely have to recommend something by that great African leader and scholar, Shaykh Uthman

Dan Fodio. Many Muslims will be surprised when they find out who he was, what he did and the clarity of his teachings. My personal favourite is a compilation published as "A Handbook on Islam" which is exactly as it says, a very small handbook for Muslims telling them all they need to know to carry out there duties. It's as relevant to the new Muslim as it is to those who have been Muslims all there lives, and this is a pure teaching coming straight out of West Africa.

I would then have to go for one of the Black Stone publications probably "The Next Step." It is actually a book which was sent to me from the Amir of the Caribbean community in London a month or so ago. It contains all the papers that were delivered at a conference they had recently entitled The Next Step. The beauty of it is that these men follow the exact path of Shaykh Uthman and it is all totally relevant to today's situation here in America, in England, in Africa and wherever you find our people. The book highlights the need for individuals to recognise their Creator, come together and strive to establish something positive. It also shows the level of conspiracy, slander and even torture that these people will undoubtedly face in establishing justice in the land.

Now assuming that your listeners have read all the biographies I could recommend my final choice would have to be a book by a dear friend of mine born in Zambia but also living in England, by the name of Ahmad Thompson. He has written many very informative books which should all be read if possible, but I would especially recommend one entitled "Dajjal." At the moment copies of that book are like gold dust but I expect the publishers will do another reprint soon because of the demand. When you read this book the first time some of the revelations seem hard to believe but they are actually very easy to verify or confirm. Then you begin to see the country we live in for what it actually is.

Gus: That sounds like a very interesting selection and I look forward to the usual comments from those listeners that take up the challenge. Now I noticed that you mentioned a man by the name of Shaykh Uthman Dan Fodio and I know that you have actually changed your name to Uthman Malik Abdal Hakim. Is there a connection?

X: Most definitely.

Gus: Before you explain that connection let me point out to the listeners that the second part of your name is Malik and we all know that Malcolm X later became know as Malik Shabazz, maybe you could explain the whole importance of names in traditional African and Muslim societies?

X: I don't want to portray the image that names and style of dress and things like this as being all important when there are so many other serious matters to address, but how we name our children says a lot about who we are and with Muslims the first things we like to portray is our love of our Creator, Allah. Hence all the names beginning with "Abdal" which means slave or servant of. That is why you have Abdal Hakim, slave of The Wise or Abdal Rahman slave or The Merciful and of course Abdallah, slave of Allah. These are all names or attributes of Allah and the Muslim is pleased to be the slave of Allah, and no one else.

The word Malik means King or Owner but it is also the name of one of great scholars, the great Imam Malik of Madina. The significance of this is that the true fully blown practice of Islam was there in Madina 1400 years ago and it was the best community ever seen on the face of the earth, but like all communities and civilisations it has its high point and then it declines. What Imam Malik did was to record that high point that had been transmitted to, and practiced by, the companions of the Prophet Muhammad peace be upon him, before it declined. What he recorded in his book called "Al Muwatta" is the purest source of Islam available today. The methods he described are what established justice in North Africa and all over West Africa and this teaching is being continued in Northern Nigeria today and also by the groups already mentioned, and no one, Muslim, or non Muslim can pinpoint a more just society or system of governance.

Uthman was one of the first and closest advisors of the Prophet peace be upon him and was also the name of the great already mentioned Shaykh from West Africa who against all odds fought to establish just governance. Like the Prophet peace be upon him he combined the roles of spiritual teacher and military leader. He also died at the same age of sixty three.

Gus: What you have just told me is truly remarkable, for in my own experience the only name I usually hear connecting Africa to Islam is Bilal.

X: Yes Bilal, may Allah be pleased with him, was a very

remarkable man and was one of the earliest people to recognise the prophecy of Muhammad peace be upon him and many of the common Muslim practices today have come through Bilal, may Allah be pleased with him.

Gus: So is this all new information just discovered or what, or has there been some form of cover up conspiracy?

X: I would say that a pure transmission of what Islam teaches is directly opposed to the existent power system that dominates the world today in almost every way. So these dominant forces cannot stop people becoming Muslims just as I cannot make anyone become a Muslim. Therefore through the means of manipulation available to them through their control of the media and economic resources they ensure that we are taught a passive Islam with no teeth which is not the Islam of change or progress,and those who oppose this and recognise what's going on are either branded as Muslim fundamentalists, jailed or killed. Otherwise they are despised by the powers that be and disbelieved by other Muslims to such an extent that they are branded as insane and either locked up or discredited to such an extent no one takes them seriously.

Gus: It seems you are saying that a pure Islam is dialectically opposed to the current national and world power system? But let's take another break before you answer that.

The Role of the Market in any Future African Economy

(Adapted from an article first published in Journeyman's Review October and later in Alarm Magazine)

Building Sound Economic Foundations (part 2)

The role of the 'Free and Open Market' in any future African Economy

Market* A public place, whether an open space or building in which cattle, provisions etc; are exposed for sale;

Fish Market A market or part of a market set aside for the buying and selling of fish and or products related to fish.

Brixton Market A market or group of individual markets in that part of South London known as Brixton and subject to the laws and bye laws in effect in that area.

African Market ....?

(* Oxford English Dictionary Definition)

There is something wrong with the concept of the supermarket. Yet it is easy to accept all the arguments put forward about convenience, cheaper prices, more choice and so on. To accept this line of reasoning is to gullibly accept what is in fact a total distortion of the truth. Supermarkets do not mean cheaper prices and more choice, they ultimately mean dearer prices, modern slavery and less choice (if any at all). The supermarkets must be viewed in the same way one views a bank and the bank manager when seeking a loan knowing full well that the real decisions and criteria are set by nameless, faceless people who you have never seen and they have never seen you. Both institutions present themselves as being there to serve the community while in reality both are symbols and tools of monopoly, oppression and greed.

Building Sound Economic Foundations Part I exposed unequivocally the fragility and inherent corruption of the banking system, paper money, and the concept of legal tender as tools of usury and oppression. The present article is intended to show that there is a superior alternative to the supermarkets, hypermarkets, and the high street chains. It is the Open Market based upon the economics of open trade, without usury and without the need for banks. First we have to be clear about what is happening on the high street today. To call the supermarket the direct descendant of the cotton field is no exaggeration.

The supermarket not only enslaves the worker by his dependency on his salary but also by the stifling of his or her entrepreneurial potential (how many supermarket employees are likely to be asked to suggest even where to display the baked beans?). The producers are enslaved in turn by being forced to produce exclusively for one buyer, the supermarket. The producers will openly admit their hatred for the situation but feel powerless to challenge it for fear of losing any contract they may have and thus endangering their livelihood. Once a producer begins to supply a supermarket or retail chain inevitably the supermarket will begin to dictate quality, pricing and other details to the extent that the product supplied is only suitable for sale in that supermarket chain and thus the producer is trapped and unable to revert to a system of supplying the local market directly. The consumer is so bombarded by propaganda about convenience, better products (or at least better than the last new improved version), phony price wars and hype upon hype that we are in the worst position because we actually think we are exercising choice. Choosing between one supermarket and another is no different to choosing between one bank and another, it is tantamount to making a choice between one slave master and another. If all this is not clear then you have missed the point. If you disagree it's understandable given the level of propaganda we are subjected to day in day out but you have to understand that this is not a matter for debate. This is just how it is. It is not even a matter of the small shopkeeper being unable to compete for they are in effect a 'supermarket waiting to happen' and given half a chance will open another shop and the next thing you know we have another WH Smith. The truth of the matter is that the supermarket enslaves a thousand traders while the open market gives freedom to a thousand workers.

The bustling bazaars that can be found today in places like Marrakesh, Istanbul and Kano despite the traditional feel they may have are still far removed from the model that we need to recover. These places now house what are in effect no more than retail shops. The traders by law have to use the local currency deemed as legal tender no matter how devalued or worthless it is, and rental costs along with demand for space make it impossible or at best unprofitable for many would be traders to participate in the market. For those who do participate they have no choice but to pass those costs down to the consumer through inflated prices. So already it should be clear that by Open Market we are not talking about hypermarkets, supermarkets, a string of local corner shops or indeed the local markets and flea markets found in most towns and cities today. By the same token neither are we talking about the car boot sale. We admire their openness and spontaneity as expressions of freedom to trade which are shared by the open market, but they are doomed either to be absorbed into the system as a result of being subjected to tighter and tighter regulation, or to be outlawed to the margins of the 'moonlight economy.'

The free and open market is an open space (as described in the definition of the word Market at the beginning of the article) but the word 'open' also indicates that the market is open to virtually anyone who has something to sell, from a tea cup to a container of tea. The market we are describing will have space enough for anyone who wants to display their goods for sale. The open market will have every modern convenience found in a modern shopping centre including toilets, parking facilities, restaurants, transportation services and rest rooms. Free means freedom as a trader to choose what you want in return for your goods. You can exchange, barter or demand payment in gold or silver. No one is allowed to impose the currency or medium of exchange that you use. It is something the two parties agree between them in the moment. Free also means free of rent. No one pays for space in the open market. 'You want to sell? You turn up!' If it sounds over simplified that's because we have been brought up on a diet of technical terms spawned by the 'pseudo' science of economics.

Political freedom goes hand in hand with economic freedom. A major aspect of economic freedom is access to open markets under a just authority. Whether one looks at Ancient Egypt, Timbuktu or the Ottoman Empire one will always see this concept of the open market being both encouraged and protected. Free and open markets have been replaced and what remnants we have left today have been totally corrupted. Corruption in the market place is a sure sign of corruption in society. Therefore the market must be protected and rules of conduct must be laid down and enforced. The open market is protected and supported by:

- The establishment of trading and manufacturing guilds established upon non monopolistic methods of production and distribution;
- the abolition of restrictions on the medium of exchange;
- outlawing oppressive forms of business contracts;
- a clear and just authority with jurisdiction over the marketplace;
- no permanent stalls being allowed in the market;
- no rental charges for pitches.

Without a doubt any framework for economic autonomy that does not contain provision for the establishment of free and open markets is seriously flawed. The city without a free market is a city of slaves.

The modern open market will surpass the modern day shopping centre in terms of accessibility, practicality and choice. It will have both indoor and outdoor areas. Although the exact layout will vary in different geographical locations, the following designated areas will be common to most:

- Parking facilities;
- warehousing & storage;
- workshops;
- various selling areas;
- office facilities;
- areas for cultural and artistic displays & performances;
- public transportation access;
- courthouse;
- market office;
- toilet and ablution facilities.

These elements will vary according to the size of the market, climate and local customs which will also tend to determine how the trading areas are designated. For example, you would expect separate areas set aside for fruit, vegetables and other staples, clothing, white goods and home furnishing, jewellery and luxury items, catering, machinery, vehicles sales and also one or more auction areas. The small local seller and the big importer are both there and both accessible to all.

The ancillary services that will naturally evolve and also be encouraged along with the market include public transportation services, hotels and guest houses, sports clubs, places of worship, courier services, freight services, fax/telephone and email services, cinemas and theatres, all adding to the prosperity of the local community. It now becomes clear that the problem of structural unemployment disappears with the return to the open trade economy.

There are a number of groups today pursuing the reestablishment of the open market in various locations and it is worth mentioning some of these projects to give us a sense of the possible approaches.

South Africa

In Atteridgeville, a township outside of Pretoria, a group of young African men under the authority of an Amir (leader of a Muslim community) have recently set up a weekly market on common land (or at least unused government land). The sight of twenty market stalls in a black township in South Africa should not be taken lightly. The legacy of apartheid is that nothing but eating, sleeping, sex and crime are expected or encouraged in the townships while all commercial activities and employment are centered around the big cities.

Bermuda

A proposal was put forward by the League of the Black Stone directly to the government of Bermuda concerning the development of a free port and open market. The proposed site is a recently vacated US Airbase on the island. The proposal encompasses all that we have been describing. Being based around a shipping port and an airport there is scope for container, ship and plane loads of merchandise, and therefore international trade on a large scale, as well as local trading on a small scale. However the concept remains the same, no taxes, no import or export duties or tariffs. The ancillary services needed to support such an operation would provide employment and business opportunities for hundreds of Bermudians. They include fresh water facilities, hotels, security, communications, storage, lifting facilities and local agents. A sudden change of leadership has stalled the process for the time being.

Switzerland (Zurich) The European Souk

A project to design and build an open market on a large scale with room for thousands of traders has reached an advanced stage of development at a site in Zurich and is due to open in Summer 1998.

As we said before it is the providing of ancillary services and the opportunity to trade that make an area with a free market prosperous. There are no truly free markets around today. The Ottoman Empire and parts of North and West Africa saw some of the last prominent examples of what we are describing. Significantly these were all operated under Islamic governance. The Muslims recognised the importance of the market and made no bones about keeping it clean, in every sense of the word. It is that historical model that is the most accessible to our scrutiny today in terms of the necessary detail. If we do that we will see that the market reflects certain conditions in the society. Namely clear and accepted leadership, clear and commonly accepted moral principles and an efficient judicial system. It did not mean that all the traders were Muslim, far from it, these markets attracted traders from far and wide, but it was known for example, that in the Islamic market, one would not openly consume or sell alcohol or pork. So it must be clear that the leadership of all the prominent and active groups amongst us need to cooperate in order to determine common principles for our own communities. This combined with a clear political leadership will be the beginning of redefining what we can call a Black Economy. The task of charting a common way forward for the black community has been set in motion by those involved in the New African Global Alliance .

Where there is trade there are trade disputes therefore there needs to be an authority in the market responsible for arbitration He or she may be referred to as the judge, qadi, steward, sheriff or some other title. Disputes are settled there and then in the market and the judge's decision must be implemented immediately. This brings us to the question of the other personnel needed to run the open market efficiently. They would include security staff, maintenance staff, market supervisors, administrators, cleaners and messengers. They would use the common tools of their trade including computers, and closed circuit television.

You may wonder how it is that you have all these staff and yet charge no rental for stall space but we will come to that shortly. First we have to look at this question of the medium of exchange or money. It is important that we understand that the concept of legal tender is diametrically opposed to the concept of a free and open market. If you are selling a product I want and I have something you want then a straight forward exchange is possible which we call bartering. However, this is often not the case so I would be forced to go around bartering until I get something you will accept in exchange for what I want from you. The solution is a medium of exchange acceptable to everybody, something of value in itself.

In examining this issue one's attention is drawn to two very interesting schemes currently in operation, the Local Exchange trading system (LETS) in Stroud (England), and a similar system in Ithaca New York. Both schemes are aimed at facilitating the barter of products and services in their local communities and eliminating the necessity for using banknotes. The Stroud scheme now boasts hundreds of members and both produce directories of those participating in the scheme. The scheme is backed up by an increasingly bureaucratic system of debits and credits and balances not unlike the modern clearing systems used by banks. In Ithaca in particular the use of locally printed currency has become increasingly popular using local materials and designs. These schemes are now being seconded by the state which is a sure sign of their compatibility with the very system they set out to challenge. Indeed, the so called Stroud Pound and Ithaca Hour are valued in terms of the pound and the dollar respectively meaning that there is no real autonomy. Indeed the Ithaca Hour is treated just like the US Dollar as this quote from Ira Katz, an Ithaca member, clearly demonstrates:

> *"Tompkins County District Attorney George Dentes has ruled that counterfeiting Ithaca Hours would be a felony second degree forgery of a financial instrument punishable by 2.37 years in jail."*

Barter is simple and therefore anything that aids the process of barter must also be simple. These schemes ultimately do not challenge the monopoly of paper money they can only support it. Their great advantage is their effectiveness in keeping resources and wealth circulating within a local community. The prospects they offer for international or even national trade are much more limited. A medium of exchange must be something easily transferable, moveable and readily accepted. Something that, unlike our pounds and dollars, does not begin to depreciate the moment it goes into our pockets. Cowrie shells, salt, copper and rice have been known to be used in different places at different times. However, two commodities have always remained universally acceptable up until the present day, namely gold and silver.

There are communities around the world, including this country, who are minting gold and silver coins and who use them when they trade amongst themselves. Our leaders, and every responsible man and woman, must take it upon themselves to grasp the enormous significance of this. There are people amongst us familiar with these issues and who are involved in the distribution and use of these coins. They understand this crime of usury and how it affects our community, and that understanding is something we all need to take on as a matter of priority.

The other important building block is the formation of Traders Associations and ultimately the restoration of the Traders and Manufacturers Guilds. It is elimination of usurious trading practices and implementation of just and fair business contracts that will enable the traders to fulfil their historical, fundamental, economic and social roles. Unfortunately a fuller examination of this subject is beyond the scope of the present article.

Let us now look at the market in operation and some of the rules that have to be upheld which include:

- Only selling in the designated trading areas;
- no selling from workshops, offices or store rooms;
- all trading must be open for scrutiny;
- no permanent pitches and no reserving of space;
- all stalls on a first come first serve basis;
- no selling of products deemed illegal;
- no usurious trading practices.

The market authority will only intervene if someone is clearly contravening the rights of others or if there is a justifiable complaint.

The running of the market is in the first instance financed by the renting of storage space and workshops. So in the purpose built open market you could for example have the main trading areas situated on the ground floor and the storage and workshops on the above floors, not unlike some modern shopping centres. Other income will be derived from other ancillary services that become necessary such as the rental of catering equipment and physical stalls and parking fees to the public. In the Islamic model the markets were established on free land designated by the rulers, or the wealthy and influential were called upon to set up charitable endowments for the same purpose. The deed of endowment was drawn up before the judge under the direct authority of the reigning Sultan so as to avoid any corruption or abuse of power in the process and also as a mark of its significance as a factor in urban development. It is these same institutions that would have been responsible for the maintenance of the mosques, hospitals, public baths, schools and hostels.

Free markets have been replaced by monopolistic distribution. The free markets meant the movement of merchandise for public sale while monopolistic distribution represents the movement of goods already sold. For with the supermarkets the movement of goods is the delivery of products to them that they already own. No one else gets a look in. Monopolistic distribution kills free trade and the free trader. It is the traders traveling between the open markets that constituted the old time Trading Caravans. Our own traders traveling between the new markets will constitute the modern day caravans or Trading Delegations and it is no less than access to open markets that will move Africa and the Caribbean from being some of the most impoverished places in the world to some of the wealthiest.

Today many desiring to trade freely in an open market are forced into cyberspace on the internet with its unlimited and easy access. Stories abound concerning the money made by quick thinking and shrewd traders, but the proposed future of the internet will be a 'virtual' repeat of the story of the marketplace except that it will be much quicker. The monopolies are now moving in with the sole purpose of taking effective control of the whole internet setup and we now hear that the Microsoft magnate bill Gates is prepared to spend literally billions of dollars pursuing this aim. We may rest assured that it is not a charitable endowment he has in mind.

This article has been written with the aim of propagating the kind of thinking and action that will enable us to work towards establishing a new economic framework, not for its own sake but because in the final analysis we are left with no other choice. As a first step we strongly recommend the publication <u>Trade First</u> *and* <u>The Forbidden Dialogues</u> (see bibliography) as compulsory reading for those who wish to acquire a firm grasp of the historical and economic context together with a clear tactical appreciation of the following:

- The formation of traders alliances/associations and ultimately guilds;
- the minting of gold and silver currencies;
- the strategic use of gold and silver as the medium of exchange in transactions;
- eliminating the use of oppressive business contracts amongst each other;
- the leadership of all politically active groups initiating a programme of education around these issues.

African Market: A market situated in a African community and under the authority of the leadership of that community with free and equal access to all who wish to trade without usury or monopoly within the just parameters prescribed by that authority.

Addendum: Since this article was first written a number of themed and short term market projects have taken place in many countries including the UK. It has become evident for all to see that across the world markets and access to markets are the key to economic prosperity and alleviating poverty.

The following excerpt from a recent document produced

by the Open Trade Network demonstrate the growing recognition of what has been put forward:

…We think that our concept of the Open Market can radically change and regenerate communities and society in general for the better, and in doing so directly tackle issues of poverty, isolation and unemployment. The Open Market can cater for 2,000 independent traders in less space than a shopping centre currently catering for just 100 shops. The Open Market will be able offer greater choice and lower prices, naturally support local producers, support existing businesses and be a hive of social activity and interaction.

Many reports point to the beneficial effect of markets in general on the population.

(1) Markets as Social Spaces - *Joseph Rowntree Foundation (2006)*

"..The team found that:

Markets were important sites of social interaction for all groups in the community,but most significantly for older people, especially women. Markets also represented important social spaces for mothers with young children, young people, and families with children, particularly at weekends.
Markets had a significant social inclusion role, as places to linger, particularly for older people and young mothers. Some markets also appeared to be inclusive of disabled people, although in other places this was less evident.

The social life of traders played a significant role in creating a vibrant atmosphere in markets, and in forging social bonds and links in the trading community, as well as with (shopping centre) regeneration and healthy eating."

(2) The Portas Review - An independent review into the future of our high streets - *Department for Business, Innovation and Skills (2011)*

Points four and five in the executive summary recommend the following actions:

"Establish a new "National Market Day" where budding shopkeepers can try their hand at operating a low-cost retail business

Make it easier for people to become market traders by removing unnecessary regulations so that anyone can trade on the high street unless there is a valid reason why not."

(3) The World on a Plate: Queens Market - The Economic and social value of London's most ethnically diverse street market - *New Economics Foundation (2006)*

"The report finds that:

A 'shopping basket' exercise found that items bought at the market were on average 53 per cent cheaper than at a local ASDA Wal-Mart supermarket. Moreover, the market offers particular benefits to low-income customers (that are) not available at supermarkets. They can use the bargaining and haggling culture to achieve substantial discounts. This process reaches a climax at the end of the market day where produce is reduced to clear or given away free rather than left to waste. "

These are just a few of amy examples of research that supports our vision of an Open Market.

More recently, and much closer to home for us, has been the example of West Norfolk council working in Kings Lynn. They recently offered and facilitated free market spaces for local traders in order to revitalise the town centre. By all accounts, although on a small scale, the results were tremendous as shown in this BBC news report (http://www.bbc.co.uk/news/uk-england-norfolk-19166145). We see no reason why this cannot in some ways be duplicated on a much bigger scale. Indeed our own experience in running market projects as produced similar results in terms of the participation of both new and experienced traders. ...

An Interview with Ralston X

(part 3)

PART 3

Gus: Before the break you seemed to be clearly indicating that a pure or untainted understanding or practice of Islam is particularly non-compatible with the current status quo. So let me put this scenario to you;

The Muslims and their supporters begin to recognise all that you are saying as true and begin to organise as you have suggested. Now there is a well known saying that one man cannot serve two masters. So what happens when the state says we will not tolerate any civil disobedience and decides to curtail your actions severely. Do we get a repeat of the days of Martin Luther King.

X: You and I Both Know that kind of passive resistance never really achieved anything significant. It was the actions the rest of us were taking and were prepared to take that forced them to make concessions, but to save face they publicly made the concessions to the pacifists.

Gus: So if you reject this pacifist stance are you then calling the Muslims to armed struggle?

X: I think we have to slow down a little here because there are some important issues that all of us have to take on board and it begins on a very local level. Malcolm X, myself and others along with us used to encourage everyone to join some group, to organise. Now this path is about change, so that was the beginning. The next step is leadership. You can call your leader any name you like, chairman, president, supreme commander, amir, don, anything, but what you must ensure is that you take the best one of you as your leader and people know who the best one amongst them is or it can easily be agreed. The next thing is that you give him your loyalty and your obedience and that you learn to trust him even when he makes mistakes. If he does something wrong reprimand him but continue to support him. The only guideline, choose someone who is not looking for leadership. In a very short space of time your community will be transformed and even those who don't like you will respect you and you yourself will be surprised at what now becomes possible. Then as a community together we begin to look at these things we have mentioned.

Gus: Does this leadership permeate through society, do women choose their leader and men theirs?

X: No no no. One community, one leader. When you give your allegiance to your leader you give it for your whole family men women and children. Otherwise you may end up having no more than a men's club or woman's club. Whoever takes on this task of leadership is leader of a whole community and you define the community by the people loyal to that leader. However this does not detract from the fact that men must do their thing and women must do their thing and these things are not the same although they should be towards the same end.

Gus: Could this not be interpreted as making women once more second class citizens?

X: Only by the most ignorant people.

Gus: OK but what are the different arenas where men and women operate. Are you against, for example, men and women sharing the same office, or in my case the same studio.

X: It goes way beyond that. Let me explain. The Prophet Muhammad, peace be upon him was a political, spiritual and military leader and he is the best example we have of manhood. Now it is said that the three best women who ever lived were Khadijah, the wife of the Prophet, Maryam or Mary the mother of Jesus and Assiya the wife of Pharaoh and therefore foster mother to Moses. So the complete man comes as political, spiritual and militant man as well as husband and father and the complete woman comes as wife mother and teacher. So in order for men to live as men should and women to live as real women we have to recognise our proper roles and then by taking on clear leadership we have to create or at least take a space where we can practice this way of life and if necessary defend it.

Gus: Apart from who you have already mentioned who stands out as examples of this type of person?

X: There was amongst the women Bilqis otherwise known as the Queen of Sheba, and there was also Nana Asmau the daughter of Shaykh Uthman who wrote many books herself and countless others whose names are not so well known.

Gus: Amongst the men

X: One doesn't have to look any further than the Prophet Musa or Moses, and the Prophet Muhammad, peace be upon them. They both came as spiritual leaders, military leaders and political leaders and they both brought a whole new teaching to there people which was in harmony with what all the Prophets before them came with. So any militant movement most embody these three strands along with economic self sufficiency.

Gus: Are you saying that this recognition of the role of men and women constitutes militancy?

X: Let's just say that clear leadership leads to clear decisions and a clear path, and that this combined with a clear worship of the Creator leads to justice being established as it was in Madina, in North Africa and in West Africa, and then it was taken from Africa into Spain, in Europe, and people must study the history of Spain and see what happened there and indeed what is happening there today. When the last of the Moors left Spain, then Spain returned to the dark ages of backwardness and ignorance. There is a beautiful book entitled The Golden Age of the Moors which I would urge all your listeners to read, but also one has to look at what happened to the jews who were also run out of Spain. You will realise that they carried corruption and usury everywhere they went.

Gus: I notice you slipped in another book there.

X: I'm in a generous mood today.

Gus: Well you've certainly been generous with your wealth of information which I for one have found most interesting and stimulating.

X: A friend of mine from Zaria in Northern Nigeria has likened information from books to reading a menu. He says that you can "ooh! and aah!" all day over the menu but to really taste the food you have to eat it. So therefore it's one thing reading books and having a vast amount of information in your head but you only gain true knowledge from action. So I can only urge everyone to act according to the best of what they know or believe and I hope that today has made a meaningful contribution to even one persons life.

Gus: As promised I would like to get back to this topic of economics and finance. If we are to wean ourselves away from the current system what do you suggest as an alternative?

X: It starts from community. Once people begin to gather in communities they can begin to decide what is an acceptable form of currency for them. The reality is that this step is enough to make a difference and once you put the best man in charge at some stage you will have to face the wider issues, and in fact you will then be capable of facing the wider issues and one of the wider issues will be protecting what we put in place.

Gus: In the short time we have left maybe you could tell us what your plans are in the near future. I know you're shortly off to Europe. Can we expect any major announcements on your return. In fact what are you actually going to do in Europe?

X: Before going to London I'll actually be linking up with Amir Abdullah Powell in Charleston and depending on what he decides a party of us should be traveling to

Brixton in London to meet with the community there. I think there should also be men and women from South Africa and Nigeria arriving around the same time.

Gus: All Muslims?

X: Most likely, but more importantly all very much on the path I've described.

Gus: So what's the nature of this event taking place in London?

X: Actually the main event is actually taking place in a place called Granada in the South of Spain.

Gus: It's beginning to sound like a European tour. I hope you will get round to telling me what all this movement and travel is leading to:

X: The event we're traveling to is actually known as a moussem. It's a gathering of Muslims from all over the world who recognise the same patterns that we recognise and are actively involved in putting these things into action. It's a most beautiful gathering of some of the best people on the earth and I cannot describe the benefits derived from being there, but only Allah knows what's in store for us this time, or indeed if we will even make it there.

Gus: So this is somewhat of a spiritual journey or a pilgrimage.

X: I wouldn't describe it as such although there will be a spiritual element, a social element and a political element, but it's a lot more than that which I cannot even begin to describe.

Gus: I wish you every success on your journey and I only ask that you come back and tell us about it in the near future. Its been a pleasure and a great honour talking to you.

X: Thank you and your listeners for being so patient in hearing my small contribution. I hope someone finds something I said to be useful.

Gus: Let me quickly say that my director tells me the phones haven't stopped ringing since we've been on air but unfortunately we cannot take calls on this programme. In fact we've had one call accusing you of being unpatriotic and anti semitic, one or two calling you sexist and communist. However my producer tells me several callers have asked if you have any public speaking engagements lined up but an unprecedented number have called up to offer you their support and would like to know how to get in touch. We have also had a few accusing you of being a warmonger. Would you like to respond quickly.

X: Only to say that it's always the case that the first people to shout anti this and anti that are the people who benefit most from all these usurious practices of oppression. I mean who runs the banks, controls the media and has a firm grip on all the trade in gold and silver around the world. It's always the same set of people who are always shouting out how much they were oppressed by Hitler or someone else. I tell you Hitler was bad but he was not totally mad. If you want to talk about war then why don't they try and justify all the wars the United States or the United Nations have been involved in over the last twenty years. Then you will begin to see that plain greed has been the cause of most of them and unfortunately the bankers always seem to win.

Gus: I'm afraid we have to end there. Ralston X otherwise called Uthman Malik Abdal Hakim. Once again, thank you.

Addendum: The picture at the beginning of the chapter shows three of the community Amirs in place at the time of the founding of the League of the Black Stone.

They are Uthman Ibrahim-Morrison (Brixton, South London), *Sidi* Abdullah Powell (Charleston, South Carolina) and Hayatudin Ibrahim (Zaria, Northern Nigeria). Missing is Abdurrahman Zwane of South Africa, later succeeded by Abdussamad Nana.

Sidi Abdullah, may Allah have mercy on him, was certainly one of those who inspired the character Ralston X.

Tassawuf - The Hidden Face of Islam In Africa

Tassawuf - The Hidden Face of Islam

"There is nothing more likely to lead to gathering of the heart to concentrate on Allah than silence and hunger. There is nothing more likely to lead to dispersal than a lot of food and talk even about what concerns us. There is no doubt that the believer has few words and a lot of action. He will certainly have few words and much action since silence results in reflection. Reflection is an action of the heart. An atom's worth of the action of the heart is better than mountains of the actions of the limbs. It has come in tradition, 'An hour of reflection is better than seventy years of 'ibada' (acts of worship)."

(The Darqawi Way)

We may not know on what those in Hollywood base their model of the extremely wise yet blissfully ignorant character on top of a mountain and full of words of wisdom. However in real life the man who turns his back on worldly affairs does exist. He is a man of tassawuf, a sufi, but the sufis we should be looking out for and striving to become are not necessarily instantly recognisable. Outwardly they may look like you and I, inwardly they may be oceans apart. We may get a clue to who they are because of their impeccable behaviour, their service to other people, the sound advice they utter or their unwavering faith and obedience to God, but it is much more likely that when we do encounter these people we are totally unaware. In our ignorance we may even view them as enemies of 'the cause.'

The language of tassawuf is a very fine and subtle

language indeed, understood by few, though many wise sayings are attributed to the sufis of the East. It has always been the tradition of these people of tassawuf to turn their attention to what they call the "unveiling of the inner eye." It is a matter of the heart caught up in the battle between the ruh (spirit) and the self along with its appetites. This is an attempt to give an insight into the role of tassawuf or sufism in Islam *particularly in Africa and amongst Africans at home and abroad.*

Any serious student of Islamic or West African history cannot fail to be aware of the exploits of the great Fulani Shehu (Shaykh) Uthman dan Fodio or Shehu Usman ibn Fudi as he would have been called throughout Hausaland. He is remembered as one of, if not the, greatest scholars of his age and for his exploits as a military and political leader. Indeed his name means Uthman son of the learned, for his father and uncle were renowned scholars in their own right. Every age produces a great sufi, a unique man of tassawuf recognised by other great men of tassawuf, and in his day this man was Shaykh Uthman dan Fodio and it is upon one of his many writings that much of the following is based.

His whole life was dedicated to his creator, Allah, through Islam (submission) and his following closely the example of his beloved Prophet, Muhammad, may Allah bless him and grant him peace. It was this obedience to the outward aspects of Islam coupled with an inward conviction and enlightenment that led him to actively oppose the corrupt leaders of his time throughout Hausaland, while he himself lived a life of piety and scarcity of material wealth. It was this same combination that continued after his death to make the Muslims the last bastion of resistance against European expansionism throughout the continent but in West Africa in particular. Of his many written works the most popular work of the Shaykh in English is a compilation of pieces aptly entitled 'The Handbook on Islam' or sometimes called 'Islam, Iman and Ihsan' Of that compilation the book known as the Kitab 'Ulum al Mu'amala or The Book of the Sciences of Behaviour is the one that gives us the best, albeit brief, insight into this science of tassawuf.

Now if our minds have started to conjure up romantic figures from several hundred years or even thousands of years ago we have already gone astray. Shaykh Uthman dan Fodio was born in 1754 AD and died a relatively short time ago in 1817. That would have been a year or two after the defeat and exile of Napoleon and around the time the Muslim Ottomans gave the Christian Serbs the right to freedom of worship. This is rather ironic considering that Shaykh Uthman was faced with the pagan rulers in Hausaland inflicting constant persecution and forbidding anyone to convert to Islam. That was also around the time of the Maryland slave riots in the USA and for the readers of English literature it was the year the Jane Austen book (recently televised) Emma was first published and also the novel Frankenstein. We should also note that it was also only seventy years before the birth of Marcus Garvey.

Today throughout West Africa and in Northern Nigeria in particular can be found the legacy of Shaykh

Uthman. Daily acts of worship, meditation, recitation and invocation of the Divine Names in groups and individually are commonplace.

"Allah has supernumerary angels who rove about seeking out gatherings in which Allah's name is being invoked; they sit with them and fold their wings round each other, filling that which is between them and the lowest heaven. When (the people in the gathering) depart (the angels) ascend and rise up to heaven.

He said: Then Allah asks them, (though) He is most knowing about them: From where have you come? And they say: We have come from servants of yours on earth: they were glorifying You, exalting You, witnessing that there is no god but You, praising You and asking (favours) of You. He says: And what do they ask of Me? They ask of You Your paradise. He says: And have they seen My paradise? They say: No, O Lord. He says: And how would it be if they were to have seen My paradise! They say: And they ask protection of you. He says: From what do they ask protection of Me? They say: From Your Hellfire, O Lord. He says: And have they seen My Hellfire? They say: No. He says: And how would it be were they to have seen My Hellfire! They say: And they ask for Your forgiveness.

He said: Then He says: I have forgiven them and I have bestowed upon them what they have asked for, and I have granted them sanctuary from that from which they asked protection. He said: They say: O Lord, among them is So and So, a much sinning servant, who was merely passing by and sat down with them.

He said: And He says: And to him (too) I have given forgiveness: he who sits with such people shall not suffer."

(Hadith Qudsi related by Muslim)

In looking at the Shaykh's book we see that the first unit is entitled **Islam - The Science of Fiqh**. This section deals with the outward aspects of Islamic worship which many people will be familiar with. They include the *Shahada,* or declaration of faith, which is to say before witnesses that there is only one god, Allah, and to express belief in the Prophethood of Muhammad, peace and blessings be upon him.

The next pillar is the *Salat* or prayer and most people will be aware of the five daily prayers prescribed for Muslims. This is followed by the *Zakat* (or poor due) which is a yearly payment (of normally 2.5%) taken from any wealth a Muslim has had sitting untouched **for a year or more**. It is not a tax on earnings (income tax) but is only taken on idle wealth and can only be used for very specific purposes. In fact it can only be given directly to specific people who fit into certain categories (poor, destitute etc.)

Another well known pillar is the *Sawm* or fasting during the lunar month of Ramadan. Many will be aware of the physical benefits one may derive from fasting but the Islamic purpose and obligation to fast may be different or unfamiliar with what many might envisage.

The last of the pillars he mentions is the *Hajj* or pilgrimage to the Ka'aba in Mecca first built by the prophet Ibrahim (Abraham). One should do this at least once in a lifetime if capable in terms of health, freedom from debt, freedom to travel, ability to avoid war zones and ensuring the needs of one's family or dependants while away.

The second section in Shaykh Uthman's book concerns **Tawhid**, the absolute oneness or singularity of the Creator, Allah. He spells out clearly what constitutes belief in Allah and what constitutes disbelief. It is what protects the Muslim from wild claims such as calling himself a god or from likening any other being to God. It is this clarity that makes bowing to idols so abhorrent to the Muslim. This section also goes on to explain Prophethood in no uncertain terms. It explains what was impossible for any messenger sent to mankind by God and what our attitude towards them should be. Unbeknown to many is that Muslims believe in a complete line of prophets from and including Adam, Ibrahim, Musa (Moses), Nuh (Noah), Lut (Lot), Dawoud (David), Yahya (known as John the Baptist), Issa ibn Maryam (Jesus the son of Mary) and finally Muhammad, may Allah's peace and blessings be upon them all. It is this clear understanding of the oneness of the Creator and a clear understanding of Prophethood that prevents the Muslim from ever believing any notion that anyone is the son, brother, mother, father or other relative of God or has any other kind of kinship with God. Although there is no doubt that we all have a contract with God, the only relationship is that of Creator and created. Despite what anyone might say it is this clarity on these subjects taken within the spiritual path of **Tassawuf** that have always been one of the main attractions to Islam for Africans everywhere.

"...If you were to concern yourself with the physical bodies and their perfection of form and their inner connection like a string of pearls

If you were to concern yourself with the secrets of the tongue and its articulation and its expression of what you conceal in your breasts

If you were to concern yourself with the secrets of all the limbs and the ease with which they obey the heart

If you were to concern yourself with the turning of the hearts to obedience and how they sometimes move to disobedience

If you were to concern yourself with the earth and the variety of its plants and great expanse of smooth and rugged land that it contains

If you were to concern yourself with the secrets of the oceans and its fish and its endless waves held back by an unconquerable barrier

If you were to concern yourself with the secrets of the winds how they bring the mists and clouds which bring down rain

And if you were to concern yourself with the secrets of all the heavens and the throne and the footstool and the spirits of the command

Then you would believe in Tawhid with a firm belief,
and you would turn from illusion, doubt and other

You would say, my God you are my desire and goal
and my fortress against evils, injustice and deceit..."
(From the Diwan of Shaykh
Muhammad ibn al Habib)

The final chapter in the book *(later published editions)*
is entitled **The Book of Important Points** in which the
Shehu gives a clear picture of what is necessary in terms
of some other outward and political aspects of Islam
specifically on warfare and behaviour towards non
Muslims. The basis for all of this and more he shows as
being clear leadership and he says it is not permitted for
a Muslim to be without a leader. Any serious study of
African culture will show that a permanent feature has
always been a clear authority and clear allegiances. It is
only now with the forced introduction of the 'democratic
process' and the **culture of democracy** that ironically
Africans at home and abroad are left with politically
impotent leaders who by their very participation in the
democratic process confirm their own allegiance to the
United Nations, thus the World Bank and IMF, thus the
international banking network. The desire for worldly
wealth and high office has corrupted our leaders.

"By men whom neither commerce nor sale can divert
from the remembrance of Allah, nor from regular
prayer, nor from the practice of regular charity. Their
fear is for the day when hearts and eyes will be
transformed."
(Surah An-Nur: 37)

So we are now left to look more closely at this subject of tassawuf, sufism. We are immediately told that:

"Each responsible person must learn enough of this science to enable him to acquire praiseworthy qualities and keep him from blameworthy qualities.'

The Shehu then divides the subject under several specific headings:

- The purification of the heart from the whisperings of Shaytan (Satan the devil);
- The purification of the heart from conceit;
- The purification of the heart from pride;
- The purification of the heart from false hope;
- The purification of the heart from unjustified anger;
- The purification of the heart from envy;
- The purification of the heart from showing off;
- Turning away with regret from all acts of rebellion;
- Doing without in this world;
- Safeguarding yourself out of fear of Allah;
- Trust and reliance in Allah;
- Entrusting your affair to Allah;
- Contentment with the decree of Allah;
- Fear and hope.

To get a practical taste of sufism we will look at **some** of what Shaykh Uthman writes about just **one** of these topics. We will examine what is written concerning the **'Purification of the heart from pride.'** *(the Arabic word **kibr** is also often translated as arrogance)*

Thanks to the wonderful translation by *Hajja* Aisha Bewley, we are immediately reminded that we were created from a most despised fluid, sperm, that then developed into a lump of flesh and after that a helpless babe. Remembering these things alone should be enough to deter us from arrogance. However, Shaykh Uthman goes on to say:

"Pride is one of the blameworthy qualities and it is forbidden to have it. Allah said:

I will turn away from My signs those who are arrogant in the earth without right.

As far as its reality is concerned, you should know that pride is divided into inward and outward pride. Inward pride is a quality within the self, and outward pride is action which appears through the limbs...

...If it is very extreme he may spurn the other's service and not even consider him worthy to stand in his presence. If it is less extreme, he may reject his basic equality, and put himself above this other in assemblies, wait for him to begin the greeting, think that it is unlikely that he will be able to fulfil his demands. If he objects, the proud man scorns to answer him. If he warns him he refuses to accept it. If he answers him back, he is angry. When the proud man teaches, he is not courteous to his students. He looks down upon them and rebuffs them He is very condescending toward them and exploits them. He looks at the common people as if he were looking at asses, he thinks that they are ignorant and despicable...

...However, during your existence, He (Allah) has

given illnesses power over you, whether you like it or not, and whether you are content or enraged. You become hungry and thirsty without being able to do anything about it. You do not possess any power to bring about either harm or benefit. You want to know something you remain ignorant of it. You want to remember something and yet you cannot. You do not want to forget something and yet you forget it. You want to direct your heart to what concerns it and yet you are caught up in a myriad of whisperings and thought. You own neither your heart nor yourself. You desire something when it may mean your destruction and you detest something when it may save your life. You find some foods delicious when they destroy and kill you, and you find remedies repugnant when they help you and save you...

...Your sight, knowledge, and power may be stripped away, your limbs may become paralysed, your intellect may be stolen away, your spirit may be snatched away, and all that you love in this world may be taken from you. You are hard pressed, abased. If you are snatched away, you are annihilated. A mere slave. A chattel. You have no power over yourself or anyone else...

"Then He makes him die and buries him.. Then, when He wills, He raises him."

...Then you are placed in the earth and your limbs decay. You become absent after you existed. You become as if you were not, as you were at first for a long period of time. Then a man wished that he could remain like that. How excellent it would be if he were left as dust! However, after a long time Allah brings him back to life to subject him to a severe trial. He comes out of his grave when his separated parts have been joined together, and he steps out to the terrors of the 'Day of Rising.' He is told; "Come quickly to the reckoning and prepare for the Outcome!" His heart stops in fear and panic when he is faced with the terror of these words even before his pages are spread out and he sees his shameful actions in them. This is the end of the affair. It is the meaning of His word, "Then when He wishes, He raises him." How can anyone whose state this is be arrogant?...

...When he is in the presence of Allah then even the pig is nobler than him since it reverts to dust and it is spared the Reckoning and the punishment

This is the Knowledge Cure.

As far as the **action cure** is concerned, it is to humble yourself to people in a constrained unnatural manner until it becomes natural for you."

So we have to **recognise that we are inflicted** with the sicknesses of pride & arrogance, conceit, greed, unjustified anger, jealousy and more. Then we must recognise that there is no place for them, we must seek the cure and apply the treatment. It is said that the cure for anything is in its opposite. Hence the instruction concerning the cure for pride:

'As far as the action cure is concerned, it is to humble yourself to people in a constrained unnatural manner until it becomes natural for you."

Now we can begin to see the wider picture and we need to bring into the picture this term **"African Spirituality."** It is an elusive term because very few people define it in the same way. Indeed in many cases it has unfortunately become an excuse to do as we please, but that was never the African way. The strength of any traditional African community has always been the shared belief, shared codes or rules of conduct and a clear and accepted leadership. The people who travelled this spiritual path the furthest were known because of their behaviour **within** these parameters not for breaching them. Today we have turned African Spirituality, like most things, on its head. We can be promiscuous, dishonest, a glutton, arrogant or a drunkard and claim that it is all inspired by the **"god within us"** which is really no more than our own personally concocted set of values or principles.

Spirituality is no joke. We must not be too quick to call ourselves any type of 'spiritualist' if we cannot define what it truly means. **African Spirituality should be true spirituality** and African Culture is at its highest when it is led by truth. Black people must not fall into the trap of holding onto just about anything that can be called African. We see that in the same way many are fooled into talking about holding onto "British" values that nobody can agree on.

We must hold onto whatever is **best** and whatever is **true**:
- The best way of educating our children;
- The best and truest form of worship;
- The best methods of trading; and
- Choosing the best amongst us to lead us.

This brings us back squarely to why Islam spread so rapidly in Africa. The leaders, the scholars, the traders all saw Islam as confirming the best of what they already knew and understood, while at the same time bringing better than they had known in other areas.

So the sufic Islamic orders or *tariqas* are firmly established throughout Africa whether North, East, West or Southern Africa, *tariqas* such as the Qadiriyya, Harraqiyya, Shadiliyya, Tijanniyya and Darqawiyya . Without doubt if one is ignorant of the history of the *tariqas* in Africa then that person can in no way fully understand the history of Islam in Africa and its positive impact on African peoples and culture.

There are many people today labelled as sufis based on the outward practices of sufism. However in our struggle we need people who can bring that teaching to bear on the wider political struggle. We need the one who joins both the inward and the outward, the prayer and the meditation, the fighting for justice and the contentment with little material wealth, the spending of his nights standing and prostrating in prayer with his aggressive trading activities in the day. Today things have been unnaturally separated in that people think they can be advanced inwardly without having it manifest in outward action. So it is said:

"...Sufism used to be a reality without a name and now it has become a name without a reality"

We assert that true teaching comes from sitting with,

observing and taking instruction from a living teacher, a person of light, therefore a heart that has been illuminated. Instruction, reflection, action and again instruction. In this time there is no teach yourself or DIY method by purchasing the right books. You have to recognise the need to humble yourself before a teacher. It is a need that you have to recognise yourself. It is a need we all have.

> "All those who have obtained knowledge and dominion have only obtained it by accompanying a humble man. By whom I mean the Shaykh whose light has overflowed and who has brought secrets and wealth with him. If you desire lights and inner sights then copy him in exaltation of Allah and turn from conflict."
>
> *(Diwan of Shaykh Muhammad ibn al Habib)*

Many reading this will say that their own religion or belief system covers these inward aspects of the self equally. We are not claiming this science of the inner self to be exclusive to the Deen (way of life) we call Islam. However the combination of tassawuf, as we have described, along with the visible acts of individual worship, the political recognition and acceptance of leadership, the absolute belief in the divinity and power of Allah, the clear belief in, and acceptance of, the parameters of Prophethood we say that this combination is exclusive to Islam and therefore **anyone who accepts all of these things is a Muslim.**

True Islam is the Islam of the Prophet Muhammad, peace and blessings be upon him, as it was established around him in the city of Madina in Arabia. However every society has a high point and then it declines and yet the model recurs elsewhere. Thus true Islam flourished at different points and in different places. It came to Spain for a time with the Moors and it is the model of Shaykh Uthman dan Fodio that prevailed for a time in West Africa and whose legacy still survives today. It is that model that is actively oppressed by certain puppet and corrupt Arab regimes. It is fear of this model that had the West scurrying to Chechnya like rats to ensure that the victory of the "sufi" Muslims over the mighty Russian army was usurped by supporting and financing a Saudi backed candidate in the elections. It is this model that is actively opposed by the West because it is the only true opposition to the injustices of the western economic system built on usury. Unfortunately it is opposed by some Africans in the West because they have been taught to think that way by the barrage of western propaganda they are constantly exposed to, and because it clearly betrays their decades of inaction in terms of a meaningful contribution to improving the situation of the African. A lot of talk and little action benefit nobody.

"I think that knowledge is based on two things. One of them is true sincerity in word and deed constantly, without change or alteration...."

(The Darqawi Way)

Those Muslims around the world who have been betrayed by certain Arabs know that their freedom lies in true Islam, a joining of the inward and the outward. So Muslim communities in Spain, Malaysia, America and even Germany are turning to the legacy of Shaykh Uthman dan Fodio. Copies of his books are in demand everywhere and yet in a fashion suppressed everywhere at the same time. Yet in our own communities we refuse to build on his legacy for the simple fact that, like the vast majority of Africans on the continent today, he was Muslim, uncompromisingly so. We even try to deny the cleansing effect of the Sokoto Jihad on West African politics and culture. The simple fact is that to deal with Africa you will have to eventually deal with the Muslims... one way or another.

History has thrown down a challenge. In this article the matters of personal worship, politics, economics, spirituality and a clear understanding and relationship to the one God have all been explored. Places have been mentioned as concrete examples in action of the path we have described, the first community in Madina, Islamic Spain at its high point, or the legacy of Shaykh Uthman dan Fodio in West Africa throughout the last century. All of what we have written is therefore based on knowledge, not personal opinion or emotion. So in putting forward an alternative to what is happening today one must be able to say, "the system we are talking about **was in place here** and here and it is better than what we have now, and this is how you reach that point," but you cannot get away from the main point which is that whatever path one pursues will only have success if the people pursuing it are people of outward good action and inward nobility, people of tassawuf. They must also have a clear critique of the current and dominant political, social and economic system.

We call on everyone who sincerely wants success for African people to begin to bring the pieces together. **The holistic approach**.

- Leadership and authority;
- Cultivation of behaviours in society for men, women and children;
- Clear indications of what should be prohibited, what should be tolerated and what should be compulsory;
- Exposure to the people and sciences of tassawuf for all;
- Clear guidelines on warfare, what it is, the necessity for it and preparation for it;
- Education in understanding trade, the role of money and the rules of the market;
- Commitment to the restoration of truly 'open markets' and real currency.

So for us there is no contradiction or imbalance with any of the points above. The inward cannot be separated from the outward, but you have to understand that there is no way to write a simple book that can do justice to such a vast subject much less short article like this. We also restate our commitment to working towards the fulfilment of the eleven Global Objectives of the New African Global Alliance (NAGA) first outlined in the book Trade First in 1996, and most importantly to the restoration of the pillar of **Zakat** paid in gold dinars and silver dirhams under the authority of an Amir.

O Most Merciful! Show us the true as true and make us follow it! Show us the false as false and make us avoid it! Amin.

ISNAD OF THE DARQAWI TARIQA

In the Name of Allah the Merciful the Compassionate

Sayyiduna

Muhammad

blessings and peace of Allah be upon him

Sayyiduna 'Ali ibn Abi Talib

Sayyidi al-Hasan ibn 'Ali
Sayyidi Abu Muhammad Jabir
Sayyidi Sa'id al-Ghazwani
Sayyidi Fathu's-Su'ud
Sayyidi Sa'd
Sayyidi Sa'id
Sayyidi Ahmad al-Marwani
Sayyidi Ibrahim al-Basri
Sayyidi Zaynud-Din al-Qazwini
Sayyidi Muhammad Shamsu'd-Din
Sayyidi Muhammad Taju'd-Din
Sayyidi Nuru'd-Din Abu'l-Hasan 'Ali
Sayyidi Fakhuru'd-Din
Sayyidi Tuqayyu'd-Din
Sayyidi 'Abd'ar-Rahman al-'Attar

> In the Name of Allah,
> the Merciful,
> the Compassionate.
>
> Say:
> 'He is Allah, One.
> Allah, as-Samad.
> He has not begotten,
> nor was he begotten,
> and no-one is like Him.'

Sayyidi al-Hasan al-Basri
Sayyidi Habib al-Ajami
Sayyidi Da'ud at-Ta'i
Sayyidi Ma'ruf al-Karkhi
Sayyidi as-Sari as-Saqti
Al-Imam al-Junayd
Sayyidi ash-Shibli
Sayyidi at-Tartusi
Sayyidi Abu'l-Hasan al-Hakkari
Sayyidi Abu Sa'id al-Mubarak
Mawlana 'Abdu'l-Qadir al-Jilani
Sayyidi Abu Madyan al-Ghawth
Sayyidi Muhammad Salih
Sayyidi Muhammad ibn Harazim

> The Chain of Teachers
> of the Shadhiliyya
> – Darqawiyya – Habibiyya
> Tariqa
> from their source,
> may the blessings
> and peace of Allah
> be upon him,
> up to the present day.

Sayyidi 'Abdu's-Salam ibn Mashish
Sayyidi Abu'l-Hasan ash-Shadhili
Sayyidi Abu'l Abbas al-Mursi
Sayyidi Ahmad ibn 'Ata'Illah
Sayyidi Da'ud al-Bakhili
Sayyidi Muhammad Wafa
Sayyidi 'Ali Wafa
Sayyidi Yahya al-Qadiri
Sayyidi Ahmad al-Hadrami
Sayyidi Ahmad az-Zarruq
Sayyidi Ibrahim al-Fahham
Sayyidi 'Ali ad-Dawwar
Sayyidi 'Abd'ar-Rahman al-Majdhub
Sayyidi Yusuf al-Fasi
Sayyidi Abdu'r-Rahman al-Fasi
Sayyidi Muhammad ibn 'Abdillah
Sayyidi Qasim al-Khassasi
Sayyidi Ahmad ibn 'Abdillah
Sayyidi al-'Arabi ibn 'Abdillah
Sayyidi 'Ali al-Jamal
Mawlay al-'Arabi ibn Ahmad ad-Darqawi

Sayyidi Abu Ya'za al-Muhaji
Sayyidi Muhammad ibn 'Abd'al-Qadir al-Basha
Sayyidi Muhammad ibn Qadir
Sayyidi ibn al-Habib al-Buzidi
Mawlana Ahmadibn Mustafa al-'Alawi
Sayyidi Muhammad al-Fayturi Hamuda

> And there came from
> the farthest part of
> the city a man running.
> He said, 'O my people,
> follow those who
> have been sent.'

Sayyidi Ahmad al-Badawi
Sayyidi Muhammad al-'Arabi
Sayyidi al-'Arabi al-Hawwari
Sayyidi Muhammad ibn 'Ali
Sayyidi Muhammad ibn al-Habib

Sayyidi 'Abd al-Qadir as-Sufi ad-Darqawi al-Murabit

A New Islamic Money System for the 21st Century

A New Money System

"Allah has permitted trade and forbidden riba (usury)"

This final chapter, perhaps sums up the key lessons learned from the Pan-Africanists movement from the 1950's right through to the 1990's.

In terms of straight forward demographics and numbers Africa is certainly **the** Muslim continent. Colonialism and its aftermath certainly favoured the often Christian minority populations as can easily be shown by a cursory study of the places that the colonists established as their seats of power and the people they put in charge. These places that later became the capital cities upon so called independence.

This legacy means that the adverse effects of democratic rule, famine, war, unjust trade practices, racism, monetary policy and corruption have until now, and will continue to disproportionately effect the Muslims of Africa.

However, the history of Islam both inside and outside of Africa shows great periods when the Muslims ruled and societies flourished, and minorities were protected. Therein lies the solution. The Muslims need to get their act together and look for the solutions within the Deen of Islam. Solutions that will benefit the wider society.

Over the years not enough of the rhetoric of Pan-Africanism has been about social and financial/economic justice. Too many other issues get in the way, such as race, religion, education, corruption and tribalism. Once you are able to navigate a way beyond the smoke screens, to cut to the chase, it becomes clear that the real issue has to be about social and financial justice whatever system is currently in place.

Over the years there have, fortunately been some men and women who managed to come together and keep it all together. They know race is not THE issue but it is certainly

AN issue. They know that there are answers within Islam. They know that banking and finance are at the heart of the problem but they don't advocate blowing up banks. They know that there can be know social justice without financial justice.

From an activist Muslim perspective everything we need to do in order to establish financial justice and reverse the oppression and social injustices of the last four hundred years revolves around two key issues, namely: **Zakat** and **Trade**.

You will see that they are in fact the very same things that will benefit Africa and Africans everywhere. So the Pan-Africanist needs to grow up. If he still has hang-ups about Islam and Muslims he needs to get over it. Things have moved on.

1. Zakat: Restoring a Fallen Pillar

The men and women believers are friends of one another.
They command the right and forbid the wrong
and establish the prayer and pay zakat
and obey Allah and His Messenger.
They are the people Allah will have mercy on.
Allah is Almighty, All Wise. Qur'an 9:72

In recent centuries developments in the monetary and economic field have seen the introduction of financial instruments and other new phenomena (such as paper money and its derivatives) which have totally displaced natural currencies defined by their intrinsic value such as the gold dinar and the silver dirham which were the standard currency during the time of the early Muslim community.

This global usage of paper money clearly affects the way in which we approach the necessary collection and distribution of zakat and we must rely on our ulema for their ability to apply well known principles of ijtihad in order to arrive at an appropriate degree of adaptation to these new circumstances. However, the degree of adjustment they are permitted to make can never extend to the modification or the abrogation of the defining principles of the Deen or the operational parameters which separate it from kufr.

So, although the zakat of livestock and produce can be paid in kind, the zakat of wealth can only be assessed, and paid, in either gold dinars or silver dirhams. One can choose to have one's wealth assessed by either the nisab of dinars which is 20 or the nisab of dirhams which is 200. This equals approximately 85 grams of gold or just under 600 grams of silver. In common paper currency this might be between £2,000 - £3,000 GBP for the nisab in dinars and between £250 - £800 for the nisab in dirhams. In practice the value should be based on the actual cost of obtaining a gold dinar or silver dirham in your hand in your locality.

For zakat purposes wealth relates not only to money but also other kinds of property, including private personal possessions and trade goods. Therefore, it is essential that dinars and dirhams become common enough for us to be able to use them as general units of valuation, and that secondly, both dinars and dirhams be made accessible to all Muslims in order for them to be able to pay zakat correctly.

The payment of zakat on wealth does not belong to the private sphere as an individual act of charitable giving. Its collection and distribution are a matter of Islamic governance.

The key elements that are essential to the restoration of zakat as a functioning pillar of the Deen of Islam are:

a. Authority;
b. Assessment;
c. Availability of Dinars and Dirhams;
d. Collection;
e. Security/Storage (Bait ul Mal);
f. Distribution.

Therefore, it becomes imperative that every group of Muslims has someone in authority among them, which implies having an amir. If not, then someone needs to be given that authority or someone needs to take it. He must then appoint:

i) Assessors and collectors;

ii) A person responsible for the safe storage of collected zakat overnight if necessary;

iii) Distributors.

He must also then authorise, or at least encourage and support:

iv) A supplier of dinars and dirhams to the people of the community.

The categories who may receive zakat are stated clearly in the Qur'an. Therefore, it is important that the distributors are absolutely clear about these categories and who these people are locally.

In the short term the amir may have to guarantee the redemption of dinars and dirhams from members of the community who have received them as Zakat **if** this will assist them in spending it for the immediate relief of their needs. However, the more common dinars and dirhams become, the less necessary this course of action will be.

2. Trade: Establishing the Halal

Allah has Permitted Trade and Forbidden Usury (riba).

(Surah al Baqara: 274)

Allah has permitted trade and forbidden usury and the guided ulema have made it clear that the current world financial system is totally permeated by riba. Without a shadow of doubt it includes the banking system, the financial institutions, the stock exchanges, the very money we use and more often than not the actual forms of business contract as well as the transactions themselves.

It is reported that the Messenger of Allah, peace be upon him, said that usury (*riba*) is at least seventy times worse than committing incest with your own mother in the Ka'bah.

The definition of usury is: An unjustified increment over the counter value.

It means simply that once the price or value of something is agreed then that cannot be increased without good reason. A delay in paying for goods or services is not a valid reason.

Natural Trade

A purchases cocoa from **B** for $100 in Kano, **A** travels on to Cape Town and sells his cocoa to **C** for $150, the result is $50 gross profit.

Usurious Trade

A does not have any money so **B** says to him, "I will sell you 100kg worth of cocoa now, and you can repay me 150kg worth in two weeks." Here there is only one completed transaction, the sale, and for the delay in payment **B** surcharges **A** 50kg over and above the established value of the goods.

B has made his gains in one transaction only, he has eliminated the natural element of risk and he has done no work. His excuse for charging 50% over the value of the goods is that the payment is delayed. If **B** continues to sell like this he increases his stock by half every time he performs a sale. He disposes with the need to both buy and sell in the normal way. In this way the natural cycle of purchase and sale is broken, this is the effect of usury. The usurer takes in and does not give out, he consumes the life blood of the community without returning anything to it, his activity is parasitical. It is for this reason that every civilisation with the exception of the present one has always criminalised the practice of usury and shunned the usurer.

Usury occurs when:

i)   Commodities are treated in a manner contrary to their nature, such as renting food, money (i.e. bank loans) or any other commodity which is consumed by its use;

ii)   Unnatural restrictions are placed upon the marketplace. These include monopolies imposed by law such as copyrights, patents and the concept of 'legal tender,' all of which open the door to the artificial manipulation of prices;

iii) There is no fair exchange of value for value. This means that the exchange is not based upon the free and autonomous assessment of both parties involved. The emphasis must be on 'value for value', the time factor introduced by delayed payment does not affect the value of the goods at the moment of exchange.

Legally we are obliged to accept bits of printed paper for our work and whatever we produce. This is usury, this is not a fair exchange. The Banks, stock exchanges, insurance companies and the money we are forced to use are all institutions of riba. An Islamic bank is no more halal than Islamic whiskey or Islamic fornication.

Without a doubt the trading practices that have always been one of our great forces for da'wa have been eroded and clearly have to be recovered.

Just as the leaders of the current usurious world economy are now introducing *(have now introduced)* the Euro along with all the trading and fiscal arrangements necessary to reinforce their usurious objectives, so too must the Muslims prepare themselves for the reintroduction of the Gold Dinar.

Muslim community leaders and scholars must take responsibility for the initial work in raising awareness of these issues and giving appropriate advice and instruction, but it is the Muslim entrepreneurs who must spearhead the campaign to make the dinar and dirham a reality in our everyday lives. They have to re-educate and prepare themselves to implement methods of trading that fall **within** the Shariah and be foremost in supporting the proper collection and distribution of zakat. It is the Muslim trader who must begin to accept both gold dinars and silver dirhams in payment for goods and services, and persuade their own suppliers to also accept them in payment.

Over the past several years a great deal of work has already been done, and continues to be done, in developing a practical and strategic programme of action for implementing what has been outlined here. Much of this will be described in the following sections.

3. The Islamic Money System

In order to make the dinar and dirham real established currency (rather than purely symbolic) then certain institutions and also certain safeguards need to be in place. It is therefore necessary to define the major institutions and concepts to which we will be constantly referring and which form some of the strategic elements necessary in enabling us to fulfil the task ahead.

The three key institutions of a revitalised Islamic Money System are:

    i)   The Islamic Mint

    ii)   The Islamic Wakala (and Wadiah)

    iii) Office of the Muhtasib

There is a fourth, and very technological element that has a major role to play at this time:

    iv) Debit Cards & Electronic Payment Gateways Systems including eDinar

We will also look briefly at two other important, and related, institutions that enter into the equation at the next stage, namely:

    v)   The Open Market

    vi)   The Waqf

i) Islamic Mint

The functions of the Islamic Mint are:

- To mint the Islamic dinar and dirham in all its denominations;
- To maintain the standards of the dinar and dirham;
- To mint the fulus.

ii) Wakala (Office of the Wakil).

The Wakil must be a Muslim of known good character

operating under the authority of an Amir (or other Muslim leader) and the scrutiny of a Muhtasib.

The functions of the Islamic Wakala are:

- Safeguarding and holding accounts in dinars and dirhams *(wadiah)*
- Executing payments on behalf of account holders
- Transporting dinars and dirhams to any location in the world
- Buying, selling and exchanging dinars and dirhams
- The Wakil may neither lend nor give credit or invest, they act solely on behalf of others.

iii) Muhtasib (Auditor's Office)

- The Muhtasib must be a Muslim of known good character, knowledgeable in the relevant fiqh and able to spot riba (usury) in all of its many guises.
- He is charged with ensuring at all times the correctness of the procedures of the Wakils and the Islamic Mints.
- The Wakil is simply an agent for the owner of the dinars and dirhams. The eDinar, debit cards and other payment gateways can ONLY operate as an interface between individuals and the Wakala. The Muhtasib must be entrusted with, and given both the authority and the necessary powers of enforcement to ensure that this is always the case.

vi) Payment Gateways and Interfaces including eDinar

The functions of any payment system must be:

- Providing a 24 hour worldwide public interface for the services offered by the Wakala via the internet (or other networks).
- Networking all of the Wakils and wakalas.

The Internet provides a convenient and cost effective access medium with global reach and 24/7 operation. For this reason any internet system will likely take the form of a website front end to a transaction server. The transaction server will perform the central recording and accounting services required by the Wakil, and the website will serve as an international front end for each Wakala wherever they may be situated. eDinar is the first of these (www.e-dinar.com) with other local initiatives in the pipeline.

v) Open Market

The Free & Open market is what guarantees every Muslim the chance to earn a living. Every city can be judged according to the state of (or even lack of) its market. Loss of Islamic civic organisation has meant that the laws of the market, like many of the socially related issues of Islamic law, have fallen into disuse. As a result, the traditional markets and its congruent elements such as the caravans, Islamic commercial contracts, the guilds, and most importantly the awqaf, have disappeared from Muslim lands. These social institutions formed the core of a dynamic social ethos that was unique and enduring.

It is therefore necessary to review and re-establish those laws and regulations of the market place as instructed in the Qur'an and the Sunnah of the Prophet, *sallallahu alayhi wa sallim*, so that justice and equity can once again permeate throughout the commercial environment of the Muslims. This must be viewed as the first step towards reclaiming the sovereignty of Islam. The following section (4) expands on this concept of the marketplace.

vi) Waqf

Throughout its history it has been characteristic of Islamic society that many of the major institutions or mechanisms of governance were not in state hands. They have always been the business of privately funded awqaf (plural of waqf), which were largely independent of government control. They were not funded by ad-hoc donations, neither were they institutions privately run by those who founded them. Rather, wealthy individuals would make a contract spelling out how the income generated from the waqf would be allocated to its specified charitable purposes. In this way numerous awqaf, some large some small, provided for every manner of social welfare. Both mosques and markets would be maintained by awqaf.

4. The Open Market
Towards the Dar ul Islam

"THIS IS YOUR MOSQUE AND THIS IS YOUR MARKET"

The Prophet, peace be upon him, established in Madina (the illuminated city) both the mosque and the marketplace. There can be no Dar ul Islam where there is banking or where the banks' paper money is the dominant currency. This is an impossibility. The Dar ul Islam must be a place that is free of usury or riba (or at least severely restricted) and a place where the zakat and the jizya are collected.

There can be local Amirs but no Khalif without a Dar ul Islam. One of the first stages of bringing together the elements that are necessary for a Dar ul Islam is the Islamic Market. In fact it is more fitting to say the "free and open market" but in this case under the authority of Muslim leadership.

In many instances Muslims would be better served by the building of markets rather than the building of more mosques at this time. The impact on the life and welfare of the Muslims would extend into social and political dimensions far beyond the scope of mosque centered activity. It is true that present circumstances would make it difficult to implement the rules and laws of the market as they should be in their totality, but this is no different in the mosques. In the West many mosque committee chairmen already have to appease local authorities upset about hearing the adhan calling the believers to prayer, and in many instances mosque premises are rented or leased from non Muslims.

In examining the free and open Market we must not become confused or be put off by the term 'market.' Even in its limited form the Islamic Open Market will surpass the modern day shopping centre in terms of accessibility, facilities, practicality and choice. Although the exact layout will vary in different geographical locations, the following designated areas will be common to most:

- Parking facilities;
- warehousing & storage;
- workshops;
- various selling areas;
- office facilities;
- areas for cultural and artistic displays and performances;
- public transportation access;
- courthouse;
- market office;
- toilet and ablution facilities;
- loading bays;
- mosque/prayer areas.

These elements will vary according to the size of the market, climate and local customs which will also tend to determine how the trading areas are designated. For example, you would expect separate areas set aside for fruit, vegetables and other staples, clothing, white goods and home furnishing, jewellery and luxury items, catering, machinery, vehicle sales and auction areas. The small local seller and the big importer are both there (though not necessarily side by side) and both accessible to everyone.

The essential elements of any Open Market are:

- no rental charges for pitches or selling space;
- only selling in the designated trading areas;
- no selling from workshops, offices or store rooms;
- all trading must be open to scrutiny;
- no permanent pitches, shops or stalls and no reserving of space;
- all stalls/selling space allocated on a first come first

served basis;
- no selling of products deemed illegal;
- no usurious trading practices;
- the free use of dinars and dirhams and any other real currency.

The market authority will only intervene if someone is clearly contravening the rights of others or if there is a justifiable complaint.

The political, economic and strategic importance of Muslims being in control of trade distribution channels nationally and internationally should not be underestimated and is an essential element. Not to mention the impact locally of facilitating new and existing small businesses and creating opportunities for individual employment and entrepreneurship,

5. Priority Objectives

1. The minting of gold dinars and silver dirhams to the specifications of the Shariah as they were used in Madina al Munawwarah must be implemented.

2. Wherever there are Muslim communities, dinars and dirhams must be made accessible to all.

3. Muslim leaders must take on the responsibilities of office i.e. the collection and local distribution of zakat in accordance with the sunnah using dinars and dirhams.

4. Muslim traders and business people must take real steps to introduce gold dinars and silver dirhams into their commercial transactions.

5. Muslim traders must actively initiate and/or support local efforts to set up an open markets under clear Muslim authority.

6. Muslims with personal savings or investments in banks, building societies, shares, bonds or other such instruments should convert them into gold dinars or other gold products.

7. All institutions in the control of Muslims should begin to hold funds in Islamic Gold Dinars (IGD) and Islamic Silver Dirhams (ISD).

8. All trustees or administrators of any charity purporting to collect zakat should begin to examine the possibilities of establishing themselves as Islamic awqaf for the support of:

  a) the minting of dinars and dirhams

  b) the distribution of dinars and dirhams

  c) the setting up of open markets under Muslim control; and

  d) a worldwide campaign for the promotion of the Gold Dinar (and Silver Dirham).

6. Implementation

After so boldly stating what our objectives should be it seems only fitting that we map out a possible route for achieving or implementing each of those objectives, namely;

i) Collection and Distribution of Zakat

ii) Minting, Buying and Selling Coins/Kiosks

iii) Trading with Dinars and Dirhams (or other gold & silver currencies

iv) Establishing an Open Market

v) Supporting Da'wa

Collection and Distribution of Zakat

When all the following points converge then the collection of the zakat must go ahead:

- The Amir or person in authority has announced the imminent collection of the zakat;
- Assessors have been appointed who know how to assess the zakat correctly;
- The availability of dinars and dirhams through a local supplier;
- A Bait ul Mal for safeguarding collected zakat when necessary, and from where it can be distributed;
- The Amir and appointed distributors are familiar with the categories that are allowed to receive zakat and will have been informed of who fits these categories locally (this will be constantly updated by the assessors).

Therefore, every Muslim not himself in authority must place himself under a Muslim authority, and must exert pressure on that authority to implement the above process.

This is the first step towards a revived Islam and must be supported by the widespread circulation and usage of dinars and dirhams as real currency amongst all Muslims.

ii) Minting, Buying and Selling Coins/Kiosks

The Islamic Mint or Ayn Gold (www.ayngold.com) can be contacted to offer technical and other advice to anyone interested in minting their own coins or purchasing large quantities of dinars.

If an individual takes up the responsibility of supplying dinars and dirhams for public purchase then it should be made clear to him that in the short term he may have to redeem some of the coins from those who have received them as part of the distribution of the zakat. This is because it is of paramount importance that zakat recipients are not prevented from deriving the benefit intended by Allah, of being able to spend it on their needs without the restrictions which are bound to result until the dinar has sufficient circulation as an accepted medium of exchange.

The Islamic Mint, eDinar and the Open Trade Network will all support the setting up of **Gold Kiosks** in local communities, thus empowering local people to buy and sell dinars, facilitate international money transfers, open accounts and facilitate other commercial and monetary transactions. It is envisaged that such kiosks might operate as part of an existing business much as one might see a foreign exchange bureau in a travel agent or a Western Union agency in a post office or local shop.

If individual suppliers cannot be found and there is no waqf, then a revolving fund could be established and donations solicited in order to have the necessary dinars and dirhams available. In this case then someone should be appointed to sell the dinars and dirhams. The size of the fund and the amount of coins that should be bought will depend on the size and characteristics of each individual community.

The standard specifications for the dinar and dirham are as follows:

Name of Coin	Material	Weight
Dinar	22 Carat Gold	4.25 grams
Dirham	Fine Silver	2.975 grams (normally minted at 3g)
Ten Dirham	Fine Silver	29.75 grams (normally minted at 30g)
Fals/Fulus	Probably Copper	n/a

iii) Trading with Dinars and Dirhams

A Muslim Trade Network needs to be established amongst those who are able and willing to use gold dinars and silver dirhams when possible in their commercial transactions. The network must consist of:

a) Retailers who sell direct to the public;
b) Wholesalers and Distributors who sell to trade customers;

c) Importers and Exporters;
d) Manufacturers & Producers;
e) Service Providers including utilities and professional services.

The immediate issues that should form the basis of the formation of the network are:

i)   Establishing non usurious business contracts;
ii) Making and accepting payments in dinars and dirhams;

iii) Paying zakat on stock and monetary assets.

A series of events examining these issues is already underway. Anyone wishing to take part or play a role in the Muslim Trade Network should contact the Open Trade Network (www.opentrade.org.uk). Local events to introduce the dinar need to be continually organised and potential organisers or anyone who can offer assistance needs to come forward and contact the Open Trade Network with possible dates and venues.

iv) Establishing an Open Market

The Islamic Market cannot exist in its true form in the land of kufr. However, it is incumbent upon us to strive to setup something as close to the real thing as possible, not unlike the current efforts being made in Zurich. It will then be the main protection for whatever headway has been made in circulating the dinar and dirham on a wide scale. The market will be a great da'wa in that it will provide trade opportunities for Muslims and non Muslims alike.

If we can achieve much of the above then we will have gone a long way towards establishing a sustainable Open Market. A simple but large warehouse with ample parking space and loading areas might be all that is initially needed in terms of location.

However, what will really bring customers to the market is choice and the 'smell' of bargains. Therefore, we should target as priorities for the market:

1. Various service providers (e.g. shipping agents, airlines, shoemakers, dressmakers);

2. Growers or major importers of key staples (e.g. rice, potatoes)

3. Manufacturers or distributors of strategic or popular products (e.g. mobile phones, computers, furniture)

In connection with the above the following points should be noted:

- Before these people commit to supporting the market they should ideally already be doing at least some of their trade in dinars and dirhams (even using an electronic or card interface) and of course they should be amongst those paying the zakat correctly to a local leader.

- Without a waqf the project of creating a market will need to be approached as a commercial venture. In the beginning it is likely that selling or stall space might have to be paid for, but this should be eroded as the market begins to pay for itself by renting storage space and equipment, providing other ancillary services, or the establishment of one or more awqaf.

- A buyer and seller of dinars and dirhams will have to be on site and the public encouraged to change their money on arrival. Prices in dinars and dirhams will not pose a problem to members of the public who will in the short term simply relate it to their local currency in the way one does when traveling in a foreign country.

If the necessary funds cannot be raised locally, a proposal should be submitted to the Open Trade Network who will endeavor to enlist the support of potentially interested third parties. Wealthy local Muslims should also be approached with a view to setting up a waqf or donating to support the market or parts of the market.

v) Supporting Da'wa

- Our Da'wa is Dar ul Islam
- Our Sword is the Gold Dinar
- Our Shield is the Pillar of Zakat
- Our Victory is by Allah.

Everything mentioned supports the movement towards the re-establishment of a place for the Deen of Islam, whether in Europe, the Americas, Africa, Asia or elsewhere. Efforts to establish a Dar Al Islam in Europe are *(were at that time)* currently firmly focused on Albania. Fifty years of communism may have had a devastating effect on Islam in Albania but at the same time the banks and other western institutions have also given it a wide berth. This means there is tremendous potential to do meaningful work establishing institutions free of the usurious banking system.

Despite the commendable efforts of many Muslim and even non Muslim volunteers and field workers we must not allow other so called humanitarian organisations (even the Islamic ones) to distract us from doing the real work that is necessary, which involves setting up trade links and financial safeguards based on non usurious principles and with the dinar and dirham as the standard medium of exchange. The other necessity is of course the proper collection and distribution of zakat not just in Albania but in places like Zamfara and the rest of Northern Nigeria where people have clearly shown they wish to see the Deen of Islam properly in place.

Addendum: In the years since we first minted the first modern Islamic Silver Dirham coins a lot has changed. Both the Silver Dirham and Islamic Gold Dinar have been minted in several countries.

By and large people have followed the standards of the World Islamic Mint (WIM) but not everyone. This in itself is somewhat of a victory but only a small one.

There are three main reasons for producing the Islamic Gold Dinar and Islamic Silver Dirham coins. They are:

1. To Abandon Riba/Usury - This means simply turning away from the usuriously produced paper and banking money and using something tangible.

2. For Zakat - Zakat on wealth should be assessed in Islamic Gold Dinars or Islamic Silver Dirhams and paid with the same or with other gold and silver.

3. To Establish Halal Trade.

Unfortunately problems have occurred when some people have minted both Gold Dinars and Silver Dirhams with no interest in it's application for Zakat but have mainly seen it as a product or merchandise that can be readily sold to Muslims and others.

The minted and distribution of gold and silver coins is in reality the responsibility of a Muslim leader and funded by the Bait ul Mal or a Waqf/Awaf,

The position we find ourselves in around the world is that Muslim Activists have taken on the responsibility and funded it privately which means there is then a requirement to become financially viable or at least break even. This is certainly much better than doing nothing at all and those who have taken up the challenge are to be commended for their efforts.

However for future success we need awqaf and Muslim charities to urgently take on the responsibility and costs of minting and distributing Muslim gold and silver coinage for both zakat and trade, but also to abandon the evil,of riba as Allah has commanded.

This is the new and continuing challenge!

New African Global Alliance

The New African Global Alliance was an early initiative of the League of the Black Stone with an aim is to unify peoples of the Black/African diaspora around the implementation of eleven Global Objectives.

The Global Objectives were first outlined in the publication Trade First and via consultation with a number of active groups and individuals were amended as follows.

1: 'The harnessing together of the combined intellectual, economic and political strengths of our most active pro-African movements from our African centred, Pan-Africanist, Islamic and other nationalist traditions.'

2: 'The establishment of a powerful international Open Trade Economy and a permanent culture of political autonomy for all Africans.'

3: 'The establishment of Open Trade Markets in our major population centres and in any other strategic location.'

4: 'The formation and facilitation of trading partnerships and the movement of real currency and merchandise within and between communities'

5: 'The development of an independent international freight and passenger transportation capability by air, land and sea.'

6: 'The publication of an independent international newspaper of mass circulation aimed at extending influence, raising support and encouraging participation.'

7: 'The regular publication and dissemination of material

aimed at propagating the work of the foremost exponents of open trade economics, political analysis, African history and African ecology'

8: 'The development of a capacity to exert influence upon national and international agencies of government, economic development and trade.'

9: 'The formation and support of Black-led organisations and agencies promoting education, health, wealth, self-determination and self-defence'

10: 'The development of professional apprenticeships and guild based youth cadres.'

11: 'The reclamation of the Black prison populations of America and Britain and the 'captive' refugee populations of Africa.'

Pictures & Graphics

Cover Ship journeys of the Twice Removed *(design by Muhammad Amin Franklin)*

page 13 The Two removals

page 19 "Forbidden Dialogues" Cafe Jam, Brixton *(circa 1994)*

page 31 Assiya Douglas *Bsc Hons*, celebrates graduation with her sisters

page 45 Tariq Amin, Brixton Mosque *(circa 1992)*

page 53 Poster for the Open Trade Network

page 71 Amirs of the League of the Black Stone

page 81 At the Moussem of Shaykh Abdalqadir as-Sufi in Cape Town, South Africa *(courtesy of Khalil Mitchell)*

page 96 Isnad of the Darqawi Tariqa.

page 101 Gold and silver bullion bars and coins from Ayn Gold *(www.ayngold.com)*

page 120 Evolution of the Islamic Silver Dirham over 20 years:
Top: The first Islamic Silver Dirhams of the modern era, minted by members of the then Brixton Muslim community in the UK. The Muslim community of Granada in Spain produced the Islamic Gold Dinar at the same time. Both were launched at the International Islamic Trade Fair in Birmingham.

Below: The newer version of the Silver Dirham minted 21 years later by members of the same community now in Norwich in the UK *(available from www.ayngold.com)*

Selected Bibliography & Recommended Reading

The Noble Qur'an - A New Rendering of its Meaning in English
Abdalhaqq & Aisha Bewley
Diwan Press

Zakat -Raising a Fallen Pillar
Abdalhaqq Bewley/
Amal Abdalhakim-Douglas
Black Stone Press

Trade First
Uthman Ibrahim-Morrison/
Abu Bakr Carberry
Black Stone Press

Fatwa on Banking
Umar Ibrahim Vadillo
Black Stone Press

Diary of a 'Son of Africa'
Amal Abdalhakim-Douglas
Black Stone Press

Follow the Money - A Muslim Guide to the Murky World of Finance
Abdassamad Clarke
Diwan Press

Dead Aid - Why Aid is Not Working and How There is Another Way for Africa
Dambisa Moyo
Penguin Books

Treasure Islands - Tax Havens & The Men Who Stole the World
Nicholas Shaxson
Vintage Books, London

Letter to An African Muslim
Shaykh Abdalqadir as-Sufi ad-Darqawi
Diwan Press

The Bottom Billion - Why the Poorest Countries are Failing and What Can Be Done About It
Paul Collier
Oxford University Press

Developing a Free Society
Hashim Dockrat
Murabitun Press

Forbidden Dialogues   Uthman Ibrahim-Morrison
AMR Publications

Outliers   Malcolm Gladwell
Penguin Books

The Islamic State & the Challenge of History
Ibraheem Sulaiman
Mansell Publishing Limited

Handbook on Islam   Shaykh Uthman Dan Fodio (Aisha Bewley)
Diwan Press

A Revolution in History
Ibraheem Sulaiman
Mansell Publishing Limited

All these and other titles available from:
Black Stone Press & DMC Books

www.black-stone.net/books

More About the Author

The author was himself born in the UK of Jamaican parents and schooled in the UK until age thirteen when the family moved/returned to Jamaica. During high school, university and time as a very young civil servant he worked in the family's retail and transport businesses *(alternating between shopkeeper, bartender and bus conductor)*. He later returned to the UK as part of his own personal *second removal*.

After continuing his professional accounting studies and holding various posts in that profession. His first solo business venture in the UK was as a travel and shipping agent in London's Paddington. Since then he has had a varied and colourful business career that includes wholesale distribution, production of health products, computer sales, telephony services and event production & management.

All this has proved invaluable in his current role as an enterprise and fundraising consultant in which he advises major UK & international charities & NGOs, SMEs, new business startups and numerous trade bodies and organisations. He has developed and delivered numerous training courses, some of which can be found online at **Muamalat College and School of Business & Enterprise.** He also continues his longstanding practice of teaching mathematics, business studies, Islamic studies and English to both children and adults. As an author he has written several books and countless articles, and also wrote and produced the play **Diary of a 'Son of Africa.'**

Hajj Amal is the Founder of the Open Trade Network, an original member of the League of the Black Stone, a respected community leader and activist, and has served on the board of many strategic and charitable organisations in a variety of roles.

The author can be contacted via:

Twitter: @AmalDouglas

LinkedIn: uk.linkedin.com/in/amaldouglas

Authors website:
www.amaldouglas.com

Consultant's View Blog & Podcast:
www.dmconsultancy.wordpress.com

Anglia Regional Mercantile College and School of Business & Enterprise:
www.muamalatcollege.teachable.com/courses

Printed in Great Britain
by Amazon